Serve 'Em Right

The Complete Guide to Hospitality Service

by
Solomon & Prueter

Oakhill Press

Greensboro, North Carolina

Library of Congress Cataloging-in-Publication Data

Ed Solomon 12/2/25–
Shelley Prueter 1/5/52–
    Serve 'Em Right; *The Complete Guide to Hospitality Service* / by
    Solomon & Prueter
        p.   cm.
        Includes index
ISBN 1-886939-13-6 (pbk.)
        1. Food service employees—Training of—Handbook, manuals, etc.
    2. Restaurants—Employees—handbook, manuals, etc.   I. Prueter,
    Shelley.   II. Title.
    TX911.3.T73s63   1997
    647.95' 068' 3—dc21   97–10642
                                                                            CIP

Oakhill Press books are available at special discounts in bulk purchases for sales promotions, premiums, fund raising, or educational use. For information, contact the publisher at (800) 32–BOOKS

Cover Illustration

The photograph on the cover was taken in one of the 15 restaurant venues at Opryland Hotel in Nashville, Tennessee. The largest convention hotel in the world, Opryland employs hundreds of servers in facilities ranging from poolside munching to room service (over 2900 rooms) to fine dining. The various aspects of the food and beverage division have earned countless awards for high achievement over many years. We express our appreciation to Opryland Hotel and Attractions, a division of Gaylord Entertainment, for this photograph.

Contents

Technique—How and Why

The Service Sequence—
Twelve Steps of Service

Above and Beyond the Call of Service

Co-Workers—Job Descriptions

In Closing . . .

Preface

Loving your work and making money! An unbeatable combination! How can you do this? First and foremost you must enjoy people, working with them and for them. This must be your "thing." If you get up in the morning and say, "Darn it, I have to go to work," change jobs.

There isn't a person working today who enjoys being confused in his or her job. By becoming expert in serving the public, you will develop job pride and people will sense that air of confidence about you. Then, slowly but surely, you will realize, as they will, that service is truly an honorable profession.

The original book, *Service Is an Honorable Profession*, was written after many, many years of public service. It truly was a labor of love.

I started at McGarvey's in 1946 and really found a home! The food service business gets into your blood! I want to thank, Bev, Frankie, Gladys and Ricky, without whom this service bible could never have been written.

Born and raised in the business, my daughter Shelley Solomon Prueter has had the opportunity to work her way up from bus girl to manager to educator to training consultant. We hope you will enjoy her additions to the technical as well as motivational aspects in each chapter.

Ed Solomon, Author   Shelley Prueter, Co-Author
Professional Hospitality Center
36214 Dellwoood Rd
Grafton, Ohio 44044
(216) 926-2608 or
(216) 282-3133

P.S.

I purposely left many of McGarvey's policies and techniques in this book for your enlightenment to use if you and your boss see fit.

The reason I was specific is that many times, when you ask an expert a question, the answer is, "That depends." I felt a direct approach was best for the trainee or pro alike.

Editor's Note:

Throughout this manual the words used to describe positions such as hosts, hostesses, waitresses, waiters, sales hosts/hostesses, and uses of he and she, etc. are interchangeable and are not meant to denote a particular gender preference.

Introduction

Service is one of the oldest acts of hospitality in existence and is an honorable profession. It represents something special to your guest. To him, dining time is the time of relaxation and companionship. Special precaution must be taken to ensure that enjoyment of good food is not spoiled by careless service.

Hospitality service is a great business for people who like people. Much of the satisfaction which you derive from your very "being" depends on your attitude toward your work. By being cheerful and friendly, you will not only increase your earnings, but you will also be building more pleasant and happier relationships with your fellow employees.

Please read this book thoroughly. Review it from time to time. Ask yourself, "Am I a professional server?" Your tips will provide the real answer. They will be bigger and better if you can honestly answer, "yes."

Your job as a "sales oriented server" will involve many of your talents: the charm of a gracious host, tact of a diplomat, insight of a psychologist, conditioning of a nurse, and selling skills of a super salesman. Could any other profession be so interesting? And profitable?

1

What a Restaurant Is to People

If all that our traveling and visiting Americans wanted was something to satisfy the pangs of hunger, the old brown paper bag would suffice.

Good food is important, but good service is more important. It is the extra touch that satisfies the American hunger for prestige that goes with eating out, having a snack or just a cup of coffee.

We, in the restaurant industry, are really in the business to help our guests find that interesting land of adventure where they can find prestige with some excitement in life.

No other business gives customers the sense of leisure, the companionship of friends or the chance to show off clothes and personalities as well as our restaurants do.

We are in "The Hospitality Industry," not "The Restaurant Business."

2

The Customer Is King

As each guest enters a restaurant, he asks a question of himself — "Will this restaurant be friendly to me?" Mr. King and Mrs. Queen get their answers from you. "The taste of the roast is often determined by the handshake of the host," said Ben Franklin almost 200 years ago. Remember:

Your face is a mirror.
Smile and it will smile back,
Smile at people and they will smile back.

It has often been said that in all customer service operations the first thirty seconds of contact with the personnel of a store is the period in which the customer forms lasting opinions of the business.

Benefits to you for being an expert in your chosen field of work are the following:

More prestige—Guests like *great* service and their compliments are nice. Just like the doctor, you know what you are doing.

More return guests and bigger tips—The more guests like you the more often they will come back to visit and afford you the opportunity to make more money.

Personality development—The things you learn and the qualities you develop associating with people help improve your personality on and off the job. Who doesn't enjoy being popular?

Increased profits and jobs—All of our earnings come from sales. Mr. King and Mrs. Queen really pay your wages. They want and should be given expert service. The results of your ability mean increased profits for you and your boss and insure job security for you.

Easier work—Training aids develop a smooth and easy way of doing your work more efficiently.

If you as a "sales oriented server" give Mr. King and Mrs. Queen excellent service and personal attention, they will come back again and again.

The most elegant decorations and the brightest lights are only background without you. Fixtures are not capable of expression, nor are they capable of responding to human needs. You may be the only personal contact the guest has with the service staff, so you represent management and the entire staff. The guest may judge the entire restaurant by the quality of the dining room service that *you* give.

First impressions are formed by the things you say and do. Every restaurant employee the guest sees and hears has an effect on your tips. In fact, you may have lost your tip before you met your guest because of the careless action of a co-worker. You may have lost it when your guest saw your actions toward another guest. Remember! Guests form their opinions the minute they walk through the door of your restaurant. Will you make them feel like a Mr. King and Mrs. Queen?

3

Do You Fit the Picture?

Just how do you measure up for the first impression? Every guest judges you by putting you against an ideal chart made up of the way you look, act and talk and your attention to his needs. Let's examine each of these factors.

A. **Looks.** You must be neat and aware of your personality and appearance, the qualities that bring admiration and compliments from friends, co-workers, employers and guests. Stand and walk erect, naturally. We feel that appearance is so important that we have devoted an entire chapter to it.

B. **Actions.** The way *you* act is important to both you and the guest. So how about trying the following musts:

   1. Smile. Be happy. Leave personal problems at home.
   2. Your face is a mirror. It reflects your mood.

3. Divide your attention equally among all of your guests.
4. Handle problem guests quietly and tactfully.
5. Know when your guest wants to be serious. Too much "kidding around" isn't always appreciated.
6. Don't form server cliques in the dining area.
7. Take time with your guests! If they want to talk with you, don't be curt no matter how busy you are. Say that you will be back in a moment.
8. Don't smother guests with over-attention. Assist your guests if they require it, but don't make them feel helpless.

Be alert to customer needs . . . no cliques

C. **Communications.** How successful you are in communicating depends on the following:
1. Look at the guest.
2. Smile as you speak.
3. Speak distinctly. Don't mumble! Enunciate!
4. Speak with a tone your guest can hear, but don't shout.
5. Whatever you do, don't forget those "Sirs" and "Ma'ams" (regardless of age).
6. Listen!

D. **Alertness.**
1. If your guest has an accident, take care of it quietly and promptly. Try to avoid embarrassing the guest.
2. If the guest requests information that you can't supply, refer his request to the manager, hostess, or a more experienced server.
3. Be particularly alert for the needs of small children (tomorrow's guests).

There is a cartoon on the wall of a New York steak house which shows a guest asking a waiter for the time. The waiter replies, "Sorry, Mister, this ain't my table." In such humor there is painful truth. You must be aware of the refinements which make the difference between a plate carrier and a professional!

The hallmark of fine service is attention to detail. It involves maintaining all of your tables with the necessities and clearing away the non-essentials as the meal progresses. The attention to minute detail separates the expert from the amateur.

A survey was taken at all our restaurants and the guests were asked what they considered most important in the personal appearance of a server. The unanimous answer was a *smile.* All of the following will aid in your becoming that *terrific* server:

1. The smile, of course!
2. Good mental health.
3. Good physical health. Sufficient rest to carry out your duties.
4. Thorough knowledge of your duties.
5. Immaculate grooming, pleasing habits, good judgment.
6. Willingness to serve.
7. Charm and personality . . . These are easily obtained through being truly sincere. Sincerity will inspire confidence and naturally attract success.
8. Team work and cooperation are known as the buddy system.
9. Make each patron feel that he is your personal guest. Remember, they are the purpose of our work, not an interruption of it!
10. Give the guests a cheery greeting, efficient service and a pleasant good-bye.
11. Use tact, initiative and cheerfulness to your best advantage.
12. Remember, the guest isn't always right, but she/he's never wrong. Don't argue!
13. It is your job to put the guest at ease. Make him/her feel at home.
14. The professional server who makes money studies the guest's personality to help him/her with the right approach.
15. Knowledge pays off. Please remember that, just as in your own home, guests like to be remembered by name.
16. If there is going to be a delay, the greeting should include a recognition of the fact and an assurance that the guest will get service. Recognize him immediately. Don't ignore him or down will go your tip and his positive first impression. Smile and say, "Good evening, I'll be with you shortly."
17. A smile and pleasant attitude say more than words convey. Greet guests in a friendly, not sexy, manner.

18. Everybody likes a person with a happy disposition. Smile easily and let it be reflected in your voice.
19. A customer is always a guest and should be recognized as such in spite of the rush.
20. Do unto others as you would have them do unto you.

The complete picture . . . or purpose:
- Not just good food, but a meal to be remembered.
- Clean and pleasant surroundings.
- Cheerful, courteous service.
- Immaculate linens and utensils.
- Informal, yet gracious, atmosphere.

Coddle them with kindness. It really pays off for both you and your employer.

Review (Chapters 1, 2 and 3)
Fill in blanks with correct answer from this list:
(Answers are contained in Appendix C, pages 225–229)

personality	food	mumble
their needs	you	quietly
service	talk	personal problems
training	lasting opinions	tactfully
wages	service	speak
personality	name	ma'ams
compliments	cliques	smile
people	pleasant attitude	mood
look	smile	sirs
act	look	promptly
appearance	quietly	guest
30 seconds	wrong	greeting
attention	service	tone
opinion	equally	smother
service	kidding around	

1. _____ is an honorable profession.
2. This is a great business for people who like
   _____.
3. Good _____ is important, but good _____
   is more important.
4. The first _____ of contact with the
   personnel of a restaurant is the period where the guests
   form _____ of the operation.
5. Guests like great service and their _____ are
   nice. Just like the doctor, you know what you are doing.
6. Guests really pay our _____.
7. _____ aids you to develop a smooth and
   easy way of doing your work.
8. Guests will come back again and again if you give
   them excellent _____ and personal _____.

9. The most elegant decorations and the brightest lights are only background without _____.

10. A guest starts forming his or her _____ the minute he or she walks through the door of your restaurant.

11. Every guest judges you by putting you against an ideal chart made up of the way you _____, _____, _____ and your attention to _____.

12. Every good server keeps themselves attractive from head to toe. Their _____, _____, and _____ are qualities that bring them admiration and compliments.

13. Smile, be happy, leave _____ at home.

14. Your face is a mirror, it reflects your _____.

15. Divide your attention _____ among all guests.

16. Handle your problem guests _____ and _____.

17. Too much _____ isn't always appreciated.

18. Don't form _____ in the dining area.

19. Don't _____ guests.

20. _____ at the guest.

21. _____ as you speak.

22. _____ distinctly. Don't _____.

23. Speak in a _____ your guests can hear.

24. Don't forget those _____ and _____.

25. If your guests have an accident, take care of it _____ and _____.

26. Remember the guest isn't always right, but he's never _____.

27. The server who makes money studies the guest's _____.

28. Guests like to be remembered by _____.

29. If there is going to be a delay, the _____ should include a recognition of the fact that he will get _____.

30. A _____ and _____ say more than words can convey.

31. The customer is your personal _____.

4

Your Appearance

A restaurant servers first concern is appearance, but a good appearance starts on the inside. Man's ancient protective instinct is brought into play each time he gets within smelling distance of another human. Don't let your tips go down because your guest's nose is filled with an unpleasant scent.

1. Take a bath each day before work.
2. Use a good deodorant.
3. Use perfume/cologne sparingly.

A Guideline for a Well-Groomed Appearance

Personal appearance counts! An attractive you with your friendly smile, together with cleanliness, proper attire and a sparking personality may be the reason that a guest wants you to service him again.

Hair—Clean hair, neatly combed off the neck if worn longer. Wear hair spray to keep hair in place. A neat hair-do rates higher in the business of serving food than a glamorous one.

Jewelry—No hanging earrings or jewelry. Jewelry distracts from the sales talk and is unsafe. Wedding rings and watches are permissible.

Make-up—Moderate use of make-up enhances your appearance. Follow natural lip line in applying lipstick. Use light eye-shadow. Don't primp while on duty. If lipstick is needed, apply it in the washroom.

Posture—Stand straight . . . head up.

Hygiene—Wash hands frequently. This is a must after visiting the restroom. Inspect forearms for marks left by trays. Use hand lotion daily for soft, clean hands. Keep fingernails short and neat. Use clear polish. Brush teeth and tongue (removes bacteria that causes bad breath). Use a good mouthwash or gargle before going on duty to safeguard against bad breath.

Clothing—Wear a clean, pressed uniform and apron. Keep an extra pair of shoes on hand to reduce fatigue. Change at intervals.

Don't carry a pencil over your ear.

Don't chew gum! The guests have no way of knowing whether you are chewing gum or sampling the food.

Don't smoke in the dining area! Smoke only in a designated area.

5

Your Conduct With the Guest

To be a first class server, you must first learn to keep your eyes on your guests. Diligently follow the standards outlined below in daily practice. Work for perfection on the job. It will result in personal satisfaction and financial rewards.

When a guest's hand goes up, the tip goes down! Follow the old Army rule: Be there first.

Your eyes must see guest needs before they arise as needs in the guest's mind. Each time a guest signals you, he is in effect saying, "You ignored me and my needs." He is embarrassed that he must show his need to others in the party and to others in the restaurant. Guest interviews show that being ignored is at the top of more than 75 per cent of all complaints. Get to him before he sends for you!

Guests don't understand station assignments. The guest doesn't care whose station it is. He wants service! Never ignore a signal from any guest in the restaurant.

Courtesy, dignity, and a quiet charming manner are hallmarks of a good server. Do not discuss your personal problems with the guests or within earshot of them. Don't shout across the dining room. Approach the person with whom you wish to speak and converse quietly.

Notice if a guest who is being served by another server desires additional service. Step up and ask if you can be of assistance. If you are busy, approach him and politely offer to aid him. *Report* his request to his server or to the hostess.

Never point

Describe the table completely, never point, always use table numbers (see page 45). Customers do not want to be conspicuous. This also applies when referring to the location of the restrooms.

Walk, do not run in the dining room. Inform your supervisor when you wish to leave the floor and arrange for another server to watch your station.

If you are carrying a tray and a guest is in your line of route, ask "May I pass, please?" Then offer a courteous, "Thank you." This also applies in your relations with co-workers.

Picking at skin blemishes, coughing, sneezing, blowing your nose, or combing your hair are all "turn offs." The guest doesn't voice complaints about these things because they are of a personal nature and are very offensive.

Assist other servers, especially when they have more work than they can handle. Love is a two-way street. Maybe the next time you will need their assistance.

Take pride in your work and develop a positive attitude.

6

The Origin of the Word "Tip"

Did you know that the word "tip" originated in Old England when waitresses and bartenders erected a box at the entrance of their bar or dining room and labeled the box, "to insure promptness"? Since then, "to insure promptness" has been reduced to the word tip. It is our firm belief that today the gratuities a server takes home depend to a great extent on how prompt his or her service is, as well as other factors discussed herein.

In effect, you are paid on a salary plus commission basis. The largest part of your income is tips. Fast, quality service pays off. You are in business for yourself. Your station is your own little store and the smarter you work and the harder you work, the more money you will make.

Most guests tip on a percentage basis, so the higher the check, the bigger the tip. Do not hesitate to *suggest addi-*

tional menu items. It will pay off. Another point in connection with better tipping has to do with your approach to the guest. The better she or he is treated, the friendlier she or he will feel toward you and the better your tip is likely to be. Remember to:

1. Serve your guests in a relaxed manner.
2. Make suggestions (discussed in detail later).
3. Be pleasant and friendly.

And, of course, remember this: Fast service pays off only if it is quality service. Fast service is sloppy service if it doesn't include careful graciousness. Seventy-six percent of your guests tip a percentage of the check. Twelve percent tip the same amount all the time. Twelve percent don't believe in tipping at all. *Three out of four will give you more money if you serve them professionally.*

7

No Tip, Best Tip

One much-traveled salesman used a different approach to the subject of tips in an Illinois city. He asked his clumsy server, "Have you ever waited on me before?"

"Yes, sir."

"Did I tip you?"

"I believe not."

"Do you know why?"

"No, I'd like to."

"Because you are a very poor server. Do you work to make money or just for a good time?"

"To make money. I have a little girl to support."

"Then you should wake up. You spill coffee in the saucer and leave it there. You mix up my food orders. You don't give me a napkin. I have to ask for water. I waited 10 minutes for dessert and another 10 minutes for the check . . . and the check was wrong. Good service, you have your tip. Bad service, you get nothing."

Months later the salesman returned. Same table, same server.

"Do you remember me?" he asked.

"Certainly, you gave me my biggest tip."

"I gave you no tip at all."

"But you did! You told me what I did wrong. So I watched the other servers here and in other places. I read books and magazines about serving properly. I tried and tried and now I make twice as much money. I've been hoping you'd come back so I could thank you."

One word of caution! Remember, there are guests who do not tip. Why they choose not to tip is anyone's guess. It may be for various reasons. But even the check of the guest who does not tip helps pay expenses. He may give good word-of-mouth advertising to his friends who will visit the restaurant and they may tip generously. If you serve a party of guests to the best of your ability and are not tipped, do not let your disappointment show in your dealing with the persons you serve next. It might affect your service to them and the resulting tip also.

Review (Chapters 4, 5, 6 and 7)
Fill in blanks with correct answer from this list:
(Answers are contained in Appendix C, pages 225–229)

smile	manner	needs
hostess	percentage	eyes
ear	ignore	attractive
notice	hair spray	server
gum	shouting	extra service
first	sloppy	inside
being	quality	professional
ignored	signals	
tip	to insure promptness	

1. "Tip" comes from the phrase
   _____.
2. Most guests tip on a _____ basis.
3. The higher the check, the bigger the _____.
4. Do not hesitate to suggest _____ items.
5. Serve your guests in a _____ manner.
6. Fast service pays off only if it is _____ service.
7. Fast service is _____ service if it doesn't include graciousness.
8. A good appearance starts on the
   _____.
9. Wear _____ on hair to hold it in place.
10. An _____ appearance with your friendly _____ may be the reason a guest wants you to wait on him again.
11. Don't carry a pencil over your _____.
12. Don't chew _____.
13. To be a first class server, you must first learn to keep your _____ on your guests.
14. Every time a guest _____ you, down goes your tip.
15. Your eyes must see guest _____ before they arise as needs in the guest's mind. Be there
    _____.
16. Guest interviews show that _____ is at the top of over 75 percent of all complaints.
17. Never _____ a signal from any guest in the restaurant.
18. Courtesy, dignity and a quiet charming
    _____ are the hallmarks of a good server.
19. Never disturb guests by _____ across the dining room.
20. _____ if a guest being served by another server desires additional _____.
21. Perform the service if you can, then report his request to his _____ or to the _____.

8

Before the Guests Arrive

As you would prepare yourself at home for guests, so prepare yourself now.

1. Check the blackboard in the kitchen for features for the day.
2. The cook will notify the hostess of items that have run out and which items to "sell."
3. Check with dining room supervisor for special instructions.
4. If applicable, sign in for your guest checks. Be sure to have a plentiful supply of checks. Put your service number on a complete book of checks ahead of time. This eliminates confusion for everyone from the chef down.
5. Know the menu, prices, and features of the day, and have knowledge of the foods listed. How is the menu prepared; portion, trim size, sauce . . . .

6. Do assigned sidework (usually posted in kitchen).
7. Inspect your station:
   Are the chairs free from crumbs?
   Are your tables completely set up? Sugar, salt, pepper, ashtray?
8. Your service station should consist of the following:
   A. Knives, forks and spoons
   B. Condiments including A-1, Worcestershire and catsup
   C. Water pitcher is filled with ice water
   D. Dinner napkins
   E. Ash trays
   F. Place mats

Check "in and out" board in the kitchen

    G. Tip trays.

    H. Clean damp cloth for wiping the tables and dry towel for wiping the seats. (Don't use dirty napkins for wiping tables after guests have gone!)

    Each server is responsible for setting and breaking down his/her own service station.

9. Carry a lighter and use it if you are working in the smoking section. Light those cigarettes! This is another great service that earns rewards. Don't miss the boat on this one.

10. Check your personal appearance in full length mirror. Are you ready for your guests?

9

Work, On the Side

Use a detailed chart for server's side work which may be assigned by station. Some of the opening and closing work that is done is divided below. Use this as a guide to set up your side work assignments. Assign a server to each area and write the name in the space provided.

Station 1   **Dining Room Service Station**

Keep the service station stocked with the following:
1. Place mats—one full package at least.
2. Paper napkins.
3. Sugar packets.
4. Salt.
5. Water pitchers.
6. Doggy bags or Carryout boxes.
7. Dinner napkins.
8. Handy wipes (when applicable).
9. Ash trays (be sure they are clean!).
10. Tip trays.

Station 2   Water Station

1. Stock glasses.
2. Remove trays under spigots and wash drain area.
3. Wipe entire cooler.
4. Once a week pour hot soapy water down drains.

Station 3   Tea and Coffee Station

1. Clean iced tea dispenser and tray.
2. Return lemon wedges to kitchen.
3. Stock vegetable dishes, iced tea glasses and spoons.
4. Stock tea pots, kiddie cups, glasses under coffee urn.
5. Check supply of pound bags of coffee, Sanka, tea bags, instant tea.
6. Stock cups and saucers.
7. Straighten up area around precheck machine.
8. Send bar trays through dishwasher on Sundays.

Station 4   Ice Cream Counter

1. Clean overhead shelf. Replace foil when needed.
2. Restock sherbet cups.
3. Clean chocolate syrup can. Leave on shelf.
4. Straighten and restock cones.
5. Refrigerate cherries and chocolate chips (on shelf with condiments).
6. Rinse scoops and pan in hot water, refill with clean water.
7. Scrape down sides of ice cream containers and have only one of each flavor open.
8. With a damp cloth, wipe inside and outside of cooler.

Station 5   Bread Warmer, Baskets and Knives

1. Wipe out bread baskets.
2. Stock clean bread knives.
3. Empty and wipe clean all warmer drawers. Leave open. Turn off. Bring full loaves of bread or rolls to bake shop.

4. Wipe outside of warmer.
5. Stock paper napkins.
6. Use bake shop sink to wash baskets in baking soda water.
7. Wipe food pick up counter and stock cocktail forks, steak knives, soup spoons.

Station 6 **Condiments (A-1, Catsup, Worcestershire Sauce)**

One set for each station.
1. Fill by pouring from one bottle to another.
2. Throw away empty bottles.
3. Fill to $1/2''$ from top.
4. With a damp cloth, wipe outside and mouth of bottles.
5. Clean caps and replace.
6. Store in neat rows in top shelf of refrigerator.
7. Day servers will empty and refill relishes.

Station 7 **Cooler, Creamers**

1. Clean shelf, replace foil when needed.
2. Pour creamers into a cream bottle.

Everyone **Sugar, Salt and Pepper**

1. Fill and wipe salt and pepper shakers. Make sure holes are clear.
2. Refill sweetener holders with sugar and sugar substitutes.
3. Wipe holders.
4. When washing empty shakers, be sure they are dry before filling.

10

The Table Set-Up

Terms to know:

Cover—The space allotted to each guest. Ranges from 24 to 36 inches from the table edge and extending back to 20 inches.

Edge of the cloth—The edge of the table, booth or counter, with or without a tablecloth.

Set line—One inch from the edge of the cloth. All silver is placed so that the butt of each piece touches the setline. Put thumb up to edge of the cloth so that first joint bends down over the edge of the cloth.

Twelve inches are left between first fork and first knife. This permits setting plate without touching silver. A good rule is knife down from right shoulder, fork down from left shoulder.

Ash trays are considered part of the regular set-up unless it is a non-smoking section.

The water glass is placed one inch above the dinner knife. The bread and butter plate is placed two inches above the tines of the fork.

The cocktail fork will be brought to the table with the appetizer or with the main course in the case of some seafood. Once the appetizer is placed in front of the guest, the fork will be placed at a 45-degree angle in the bowl of the teaspoon.

Other serving pieces are laid near the dish with which they are going to be used or on the underliner.

When placing or moving silverware, hold by handle. Never by blades, tines or bowls. When inspecting silver for cleanliness, do so privately without attracting attention.

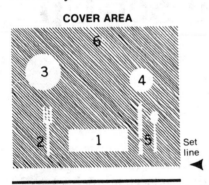

LUNCHEON SETTING

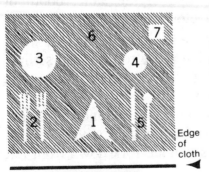

DINNER SETTING

1. Napkin, 2. Fork, 3. Bread and Butter Plate, 4. Water Glass, 5. Knife and Spoon, 6. Placemat (optional), 7. Ash Tray

Napkin Service

The cardinal rule is to fold a napkin in such a manner as to have the free or hem corner facing the left hand of the guest. This facilitates the unfolding or movement of the napkin by the guest or the server.

If it is convenient, the server may place the linen napkin in the lap of the guest. This is a done by picking up the napkin with the hand farthest away from the guest, carrying this hand across the guest's lap and dropping the napkin into place (see photograph). Never unfold a paper napkin.

Paper napkins are moved to the left of the salad plate when serving the main course.

Finger Bowls

For those who request one, a finger bowl is readily available. All you need is a small bowl, tepid water, lemon and a fresh absorbent napkin. Place the folded napkin in a bowl. Pour tepid water on it to lightly saturate the napkin. Squeeze lemon on top. Serve.

In lieu of a finger bowl, you can use a warm damp cloth or a commercial wet napkin.

Place the linen napkin in guest's lap

11

Table Service

Restaurant service is a combination of historical service passed on to us by traditional and modern methods devised to meet the requirements of feeding large numbers of persons daily. The methods of table service adopted by a particular restaurant may vary slightly from other operations, but basically the service should follow the procedures outlined on the following pages.

To give you a background in recent methods, the historical services are outline below. Basically there are five sources from which we have drawn the American service.

French Service: When this service is used, the server usually serves from a food cart or table placed beside the guest. A modification of this is when the guest is presented a platter and serving silver with which he helps himself. In both cases the dishes are presented to the guest before the guest's plate is filled. An American adaptation of this system of service is the salad cart or tray of salads from which guests may choose.

English Service: Commonly called "host service." When serving, the platters are placed in front of the host or hostess, who serves the individual plates. The waiter stands to the right of the host, receives the dinner plates from him and serves each guest.

Russian Service: The individual food portions are set up on plates, garnished, and served to the guest in counterclockwise order. This system is usually followed in American restaurants for both regular and banquet service.

Oriental Service: This service is used when bowls or platters are brought to the table and passed around. Usually the bowl is passed first to the guest to honor him. We call this service the family style. Today it is used in most of our homes and has been adopted in some restaurants.

Buffet Service: This is the most ancient of services. It comes from the Middle East and northern Europe where guests originally dipped from a single cooking pot. The modern restaurant has simply increased the number of cooking pots. Featuring buffet service on various days can be a very profitable type of business. Examples include: Friday, a natural for seafood and Sunday, great for a family day type buffet.

Counter Service: With counter service it is hard to identify hosts and hostesses. Therefore, always start serving the guest closest to the kitchen and proceed down the counter. Counter service is exactly the opposite of table service. Because the server faces the guest, serve beverages with the left hand. Place the main course (entrée) in front of the guest with the right hand. On coffee refills, hold the shield in the right hand and pour with the left. Plate removal is made with the right hand and beverages with the left.

Hand Tray Service: Used mostly in coffee shops. This tray is light and more maneuverable for the server. For food service the tray is carried or balanced on the palm of the right hand and arm, leaving the left hand free for service. With beverage service the tray is transferred to the left hand and arm, leaving the right hand free for service.

For booth service or a wall table when the outside hand is required for service, the hand tray is shifted from hand to hand as required to free the service hand. (Check booth service procedure.)

It is common procedure in many restaurants using hand tray service for the server always to carry the tray. A good server carries the arm tray as though it were a part of her physical being. When taking an order, the tray is used as a writing desk. Exception: Never carry a coffee pot or water pitcher on a tray. This is not a safe practice since a bumped tray and a spilled pot could cause severe damage.

Booth Service: When service is made at a wall booth or table, it is impossible to serve correctly standing at the left side of the guest. As a result, use a type of service commonly referred to as the off-hand method for booths and wall tables.

At a wall booth or table occupied by two guests, the server stands at the open end of the booth or table. Face the guest to be served with the side of your hip against the end of the booth or table for balance. Service is then made with the right hand as in Diagram 1.

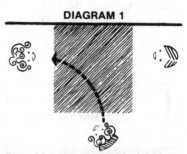

DIAGRAM 1

Face this way, serve with right hand

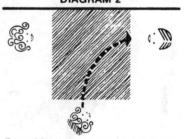

DIAGRAM 2

Face this way, serve with left hand

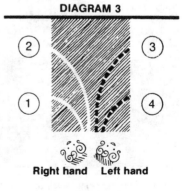

DIAGRAM 3

Right hand   Left hand

   Turn and face the other guest, placing the side of your hip near the edge or the booth. Service is made with the left hand. See Diagram 2.

Service at a Booth or Wall Table for Four: Service at a booth for four is done in the following manner: Start with the left hip against the side of the booth. Serve the first guest on the inside position with the left hand. Transfer the other plate from the right hand to the left hand. Serve the outside guest with the left hand. Return to your side stand for your other two plates. Return to the booth and face the guests on the left side of the booth. With your right hip against the table, serve the inside guest with the plate in your right hand. To serve the outside guest, transfer the plate from your left hand to your right hand (see Diagram 3 and the following pictures).

Face this way, serve with left hand

Face this way, serve with right hand

Following this system of service at a booth for four will permit you to serve your guests graciously without danger of touching their silverware or making them move out of your way.

Food service is started with the first person to the right of the host and continues in a counterclockwise manner around the table, serving the host last.

Serve with right hand

Special Situations—Locating the Host/Hostess

The rule of thumb is to serve the guests of the host or hostess first. In order to locate the host of the party, ask the hostess who greeted and seated the part who the host is. S/he most likely approached the hostess' podium to announce their arrival.

Ladies First

Although respect for the ladies in American social life dictates that ladies be served first, this does not apply in restaurant service where men and women are seated alternately around a table of five or more. Do serve ladies first at a table of four or less.

For good etiquette, start with the person on your host's right and serve counterclockwise around the table.

Review (Chapters 8, 9, 10 and 11)
Fill in the blanks with correct answer from this list:
(Answers are contained in Appendix C, pages 225–229)

five	bread and butter	moveout
clockwise	plate	left
cloth	twelve	right
left	day	family
host or hostess	menu	off hand
crumbs	foods	right
cocktail	cover	outside
food cart	prices	right
napkin	water glass	left
supervisor	bowl of teaspoon	exact opposite
light	specials	touching
inch	tines	handles
blades	bowls	inside

1. Check with your _____ for special instructions.
2. Know the _____, _____, _____ of the _____ and have knowledge of the _____ listed.
3. Are the chairs free from _____?
4. _____ your guests cigarettes.
5. _____ is the space allotted to each guest.
6. Edge of the _____ is edge of the table.
7. Set line . . . one _____ from the edge of the cloth.
8. _____ inches are left between first fork and first knife.
9. The _____ is placed at a 45-degree angle in the _____.
10. The _____ is placed two inches above the tines of the fork.
11. The _____ fork will be brought to the table with the appetizer.
12. The fork will be placed at a 45-degree angle in the _____.
13. All utensils must be held by the _____. Never by the _____, _____, or _____.
14. If it is convenient, the server may place the _____ in the lap of the guest.
15. Paper napkins are moved to the _____ of the salad plate when serving main course.
16. There are _____ sources from which we have drawn American service.
17. When French service is used, the food is served from a _____ placed beside the guest.
18. In English service, the platters are placed in front of the _____.
19. In Russian Service, the individuals' plates are served to the guest in a _____ order.

20. We have derived from Oriental service the
_____ style.
21. Counter service is the _____ of table service.
22. For food service, the tray is carried in the _____ hand, leaving the _____ hand free for service.
23. For booths, we use a type of service known as the _____ method.

Use the diagram to answer questions 24 and 25

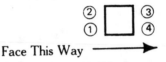

Face This Way ⟶

24. With the left hip against the booth, serve guest number 3 on the _____ position with the _____ hand.
25. With the right hip against the booth, serve guest number 1 on the _____ position with the _____ hand.
26. Booth service permits you to serve without the danger of _____ their silverware or making them _____ of your way.
27. For good etiquette, start with the person on your host's _____ and serve around the table.

12

Basic Rules To Expert Service

1. Repeat the order to the guest in a low voice as you write it down.
2. Serve cold foods cold; serve hot foods hot.
3. The entrée portion should always be placed directly in front of guest.
4. At a "free standing" table:

   A. All food service is made from the left side of the guest with the left hand.

   B. All dishes are removed from the left side of the guest with the left hand.

   C. All beverages are served from the right side of the guest with the right hand.

   D. All beverages are removed from the right side of the guest with the right hand.

5. All dishes or glasses are served and removed from the table one at a time and stacked in the other hand behind the guest. Never stack dishes on the table for removal.
6. Never reach in front of the guest with your elbow near his face. Use the arm farthest away.

These rules will give you a graceful appearance and will not discomfort your guests by requiring them to shift their positions or lean away from your flying elbow.

Review (Chapter 12)
Fill in the blanks with the correct words from this list:
(Answers are contained in Appendix C, pages 225–229)

right	right	left
right	other	verbally
front	elbow	cold
one	hot	entrée
left	right	
the table	write	

1. Never reach in front of the guest with your _____ near their face.
2. All beverages are removed from the _____ side of the guest with the _____ hand.
3. All food dishes are removed from the left side of the guest with the _____ hand.
4. All food is served from the left side of the guest with the _____ hand.
5. Repeat the order _____ to the guest as you _____ it down.
6. All dishes or glasses are served and removed from the table _____ at a time and stacked in the _____ hand behind the guest. Never stack dishes on the _____ for removal.

7. All beverages are served from the _____
   side of the guest with the _____ hand.
8. The _____ portion should always be
   placed directly in _____ of the guest.
9. Serve cold food _____. Serve hot food
   _____.

13

Tray Loading and Lifting

Proper loading of restaurant trays is necessary to ensure ease of handling and to reduce spillage and breakage.

1. There are two correct ways of placing dishes on tray.
   A. Place heavy dishes in center of tray.
   B. Place the heavier dishes on edge of tray that will be placed on shoulder.
2. Caution! For balance, start loading from center of tray to outer edge.
3. Do not place cups on saucers when bringing coffee to the table. (Nobody likes coffee in their saucer.)
4. Do not place appetizers on underliner plates.
5. Glasses, cups or other containers with beverages should be placed near the center and handles turned outward to prevent spillage.

6. Fill beverages to one-half inch below lip to avoid spillage.
7. Be sure *both* sides of the tray are clean.

When loading trays with soiled dishes, follow the same rules listed above. The maximum load for any tray of soiled dishes is the amount required for eight covers. Do not overload the tray as the damage resulting through breakage is high and the weight is excessive.

If a tray of soiled dishes is to be left in the dining room, even for a moment, it should be covered with a clean cloth. Trays should be wiped clean on both sides before replacing on shelf.

Remove soiled dishes from the dining room as quickly as possible. Leftovers are definitely offensive to the eyes and nose.

Lifting

If the tray is heavy, slide tray from stand or counter with both hands. Put one hand under. Keep other hand on edge for balance.

Bend knees, place shoulder under heavy part of tray. Keep back as straight as possible as you straighten your legs. Lift with your legs and not your back! This could save you from back problems in the future.

Tray loading . . . and lifting

Review (Chapter 13)
Fill in the blanks with the correct answer from this list:
(Answers are contained in Appendix C, pages 225–229)

one-half inch	dining room saucers	turned in
underliners	heavy dishes in	legs
shoulder	center of tray	handling
knees	breakage	edge of tray that
both	8	will be placed on
spillage	back	shoulder

1. Proper loading is necessary to insure ease of
   _____ and to reduce _____ and
   _____.

2. The correct way of placing dishes on tray is
   _____ and _____.

3. Cups are not placed on _____.

4. Appetizers are not placed on _____.

5. Handles should be _____ to prevent
   spillage.

6. Fill beverages to _____ inch below lip to
   avoid spillage.

7. Be sure _____ sides of the tray are clean.

8. The maximum load for any soiled dish tray is the
   amount of dishes and silver required for _____
   covers.

9. Remove soiled dishes from the _____ as
   soon as possible.

10. Bend your _____, place your
    _____ under the tray.

11. Keep your _____ as straight as possible as
    you straighten your _____.

The Service Sequence

The following chapters will describe in more detail these twelve basic steps to service:

1. **Welcome**

2. **Beverage/Appetizer Course**

3. **Take Entrée Order**

4. **Ring Order—Turn in to Kitchen**

5. **Serve Wine**

6. **Pick Up Order**

7. **Serve Dinners**

8. **Check Back After 2 or 3 Bites or Within a Minute—Whichever Comes First.** Refill Water and/or Beverages as Needed

9. **Clear**

10. **Sell Dessert and Serve**—Refill Coffee

11. **Present Check and Explain Payment Procedure**

12. **Good-Bye and Thank You**

14

Welcoming the Guest

As you walk toward your guest to serve water, start to smile when you are about six feet from them. Continue to smile as you walk up to the table. Stand erect. Remember, they are watching you. A warm smile carries more than words. Roll out the red carpet to your new friends. Treat them as you would a guest in your own home. Welcome guests with a melodious, "Good evening." If you know them by name, use it, preceded by Mr. or Mrs. A mere "hi" or "hello" will not be as effective as use of name. Announce the features; don't call them specials.

The first sign of good service is water on the table; fill the glass with ice water from the ice bin. Place it on center of tray for proper balance. Serve from right side of guest with right hand holding glass at base. Balance tray on the palm of left hand. *Always carry a glass of water on a tray.*

Note: Make sure that the ice is placed in the glass with tongs when at the table. Otherwise, be sure to use the ice scoop. *Never* put a glass into the ice, the glass may chip and/or break in the ice bin.

Check to see if your guests have a menu. If they do not, hand them an attractive, spotless opened menu. A smudged dirty menu is not suitable. Make sure the menu is complete.

High chairs or junior chairs should be furnished for small children. High chairs should be used only for babies. Others should be provided with the junior chair.

If two tables are seated at once, do not ignore one. Recognize them by saying, "Good evening (or "good morning"), I'll be with you shortly."

How to Properly Serve Multiple Tables

The first thing you have to know is—how to serve guests at one table—before you can move on to the second one! The following explanation will give you an overall view of how you can work two tables as one, and also attend to tables number three and four.

Your hostess will try to seat your tables a few minutes apart; however, this isn't always possible. We will assume the hostess has seated your two tables at the same time. (1) You will serve water to both tables beginning with the one that was seated first. Excuse yourself while you serve water to the second one. (2) Turn to the first table and ask in a positive, warm manner, "May I suggest a glass of Chablis?" or "We feature strawberry Margaritas." Take their order and repeat it as you write it down. (3) Then proceed to take the second table's cocktail order, using suggestion selling. (4) Go to your pre-check machine to ring the orders. (5) Go to the service bar and call out the order, pick up your cocktails and take them back to the correct table. **Note:** Use table numbers to make sure there is no confusion when you bring the cocktails back to the table to serve. Cocktails should be set up clockwise on your tray as they are written on the check. Repeat the name of the cocktail as you set it down. (6) Ask if they would like to "relax" and enjoy their cocktails before ordering. If so, go back when half of the glass is down and ask for a second sale. Don't ask, "Would you like another cocktail?" Don't use the word another. This may imply that they are having too many. In a positive tone and a "yes" nod of the head ask, "Would you like a fresh—(brand) and soda?", "Whiskey sour?" Recommend an up-sell. Repeat their cocktail or highball preference. (7) Take their dinner order and suggest wine depending on what they have ordered.

By this time the hostess has seated your third table, so while you are getting bread, etc. from the kitchen, pick up water for your third table. Deliver bread and butter plus appetizers to tables one and two, but as you do so, acknowledge table three saying you'll be with them shortly. (8) You serve water, take table three's cocktail order and deliver the drink(s). (9) Remove salad plates, or appetizer plates from tables one and two. (10) Take a second cocktail order from table three, or their dinner order as the case may be. Serve dinners as they are ready for tables one and two. (11) Offer dessert menus after you clear their dinner plates. (12) Table four is now being seated, acknowledge them and ask for a cocktail order. After you have done this, pick up dessert for tables one and two, water and cocktails for table four. *Note exception:* It is not proper procedure to serve the water with the cocktails. However, in this case an exception is made because it is more efficient and the guest gets better service as a result.

If you have more than four tables at a time at dinner, it is difficult to give proper service: Never take more tables than you can effectively handle at one time. The key to the best, most efficient service for multiple tables is to think of each table's needs as you enter and leave the dining room and the kitchen. Always try to kill two, three or four birds with one stone as the saying goes.

15

How to Take the Cocktail Order and Apply Salesmanship

The key to the selling of any item is—*do the thinking for the guest!* You have heard many times, "Would you like a drink?" or "Can I get you a cocktail?" It's a little better than nothing, but not much. Do the thinking for the guest.—"We have a special beverage for the ladies. It's called a Red Snapper and it's served in a special souvenir glass that you can take home." (Pause for a reply.) "Or would you care for a Daiquiri or a Whiskey Sour?" If they don't want a drink after two tries, they will let you know. (Know the ingredients for all mixed drinks. They are really simple to learn.)

The key to selling is to think positive! Let the guest know

that he can go first class and you want to help him. When he says Scotch and soda just ask, "Dewars, sir?" and the big percentage of the time he will take your suggestion. Repeat his order verbally as you write it down. This is basic, even when taking a food order, because it reduces the chance of error. There is a definite trend toward drinks on the rocks. If, for example, he orders a Whiskey Sour, first ask, "With V.O.?" and then ask, (if he hasn't already mentioned it), "On the rocks?" "On the rocks" means over ice cubes; a mist is liquor served over crushed ice.

If they order cocktails, make out a ticket or go to the computer to place the order. There is a correct procedure for ordering. Order as follows:

1. Wine (glass/carafe)
2. Straight liquor (shots or shot & wash)
3. Mixed cocktails
4. Creme drinks
5. Beer

(Proper garnishes and glasses for mixed drinks are listed at the end of this chapter.)

When serving cocktails, concentrate the weight in the middle of the bar tray on the left hand. Hold the cocktail napkins in your fingers underneath the cocktail tray to keep the napkins dry. Put them on the tray when you get to the table. Place the before dinner cocktail on a cocktail napkin or coaster in front of the guest four inches in from the edge of the cloth and centered between the silverware. (1) Serve from the right. **Note:** When serving a bottle or carafe of wine, it is not proper to place a cocktail napkin under the glasses. Cocktail napkins are used to absorb moisture from glasses which do not have a stem. Wine glasses have stems so they do not require the napkin. However, when serving a glass of wine with the cocktail orders, you may serve a napkin under the glass for the sake of consistency. (2) Repeat the name of the cocktail as you place it in front of the guest. As you do this, use a positive tone not a questioning one. Remember, you are not asking the guest if this is the beverage he/she ordered, you are confirming the order.

Let the guests enjoy their cocktails. Suggest specific appetizers. Don't attempt to take their food order at this time unless they ask you to do so. Build up your check and tip. When the beverages are half finished, go back to the table. Many times you will hear, "Let's have another." This requires nothing but a gesture and upgrades the service. If you don't get an order, then suggest, "Would you like a *fresh* (specific beverage)?" Direct your question to the host or the person who has the least amount of liquid in his/her glass. They will tell you their wishes. Remember to name their cocktail as you ask them! "Ma'am, Bloody Mary?"

Remove empty drink glasses with the right hand and serve the second round as you did the first. If your restaurant serves special appetizers for which it is noted, be sure your guests have all they want.

Remember, the willingness to serve is just as important as the service itself. Coddle 'em with kindness— they love it.

Be alert either to sell them a second cocktail or take their food order. Let them make the decision by asking, "Would you like to relax a while before I take your dinner order?" They will then make the decision. Remember, we make more money on that cocktail than we do the dinner, so sell them in a sociable manner. Try it. It's fun. When the guest gives you a beverage and food order at the same time, do not assume he wants to eat immediately. Let them relax. Communicate—Don't be afraid to throw the decision in their laps.

When cocktails are served with other food, they are placed directly above the dinner plate. For specific step-by-step procedures, see page 197.

Should you arrive at the table with food service before the guests have finished a before-dinner beverage, move the cocktails and place them above the dinner plate. Remove any empty glasses. Work from the right side. Then proceed to serve food from the left.

All alcoholic beverages are served from the right side of the guest commencing with the first guest to the left of a host at the table and continuing clockwise around the table. For a booth or wall table, serve the guests on the left side of the booth with the right hand and the guests on the right side with your left hand.

Note: When in doubt, ask for identification of age when young persons order alcoholic beverages. Protect the house and yourself. (In some states, you are subject to large fine for serving minors and your boss could lose his liquor license.) Just say politely, "We will be happy to serve you if you have some identification." We would rather lose the sale than take the chance of losing our license and you losing your job

Use of Abbreviations

For speed in writing and for universal understanding, the following are the standard, most widely used abbreviations for writing the cocktail order:

Liquor	Wash	Miscellaneous
Scotch - Sc	Coke - C	Twist - T
Whiskey - W	7-Up - 7	Rocks - RX
Bourbon - B	Water - W	UP - UP
Gin - G	Tonic - T	Dry - X
Rum - R	Soda - S	Extra Dry - XX
Tequila - Tq		Liq with wash - ___ / ___
Vodka - V		ie Sc/W
		B/C

Common Cocktails, Garnishes and Glassware

Ask your manager to record all your cocktail information on a chart such as the example below (suggestion that saves time—leave out the vowels):

Cocktail	Abbreviation	Garnish	Glass	Ingredient	Price
Martini	Mrt	Olive	Up or Rocks	Gin Dry Vermouth	1.50

The following are commonly served cocktails, their abbreviations, garnishes and glasses.

Cocktail	Abbreviation	Garnish	Glass
Bacardi	Bcr	Lime	No. 1, 3
Bloody Mary	BM	Lime & Celery	No. 5
Daiquiri	Dq	Lime	No. 1, 3
Gibson	Gbs	Pearl Onion	No. 1, 3
Gimlet	Gml	Lime	No. 1, 3
Gin and Tonic	G/T	Lime	No. 3
Manhattan	Mnt	Cherry	No. 1, 3
Dry Manhattan	xMnt	Olive	No. 1, 3
Perfect Manhattan	pMnt	Lemon Twist	No. 1, 3
Martini	Mrt	Olive	No. 1, 3
Dry Martini	xMrt	Olive or Twist	No. 1, 3
Vodka Martini	VMrt	Olive	No. 1, 3
Old Fashioned	Fsh	Orange Slice & Cherry	No. 3
Rob Roy	RRy	Cherry	No. 1, 3
Dry Rob Roy	xRRy	Olive	No. 1, 3
Perfect Rob Roy	pRRy	Lemon Twist	No. 1, 3

Screwdriver	Scr	None	No. 5
Tom Collins (all Collins)	TC	Orange Slice & Cherry	No. 5
Vodka & Tonic	V/T	Lime	No. 3
Whiskey Sour	WS	Orange Slice & Cherry	No. 1, 3
After Dinner Liqueurs			No. 6
Ice Cream Drinks			No. 2
Cream Drinks			No. 4

Suggested Glasses For Common Mixed Drinks

1. "Up" glass—3 oz.
2. Wine glass—6 oz or 8 oz.
3. Rocks glass—5-8 oz.
4. Champagne glass
5. Tall or Collins glass
6. Pony

Review (Chapters 14 and 15)
Fill in the blanks with the correct answer from this list:
(Answers are contained in Appendix C, pages 225–229)

half	water	4
right	customer	be with you shortly
cocktail napkin	smile	mixed drinks
identification	right	creme drinks
water glass	dinner order	six
kindness	center	water
coffee cup	liquor	positively
would you like to	verbally	wine
relax a while	food service	cocktail
write	Good Evening	left
thinking	a fresh	beer

1. As you walk toward your guest to serve _____,
   start to _____ when you are about _____
   feet from him.
2. The first sign of good service is _____ on the
   table.
3. Place iced glasses on _____ of tray. Balance
   on left hand. Serve from right side with right hand for
   free-standing tables.
4. If two tables are seated at the same time, don't ignore
   one. Recognize them by saying _____
   I'll _____.
5. The key to selling is to do the _____
   for the _____ and think _____.
6. Repeat the order _____ as you
   _____ it down.
7. The correct procedure for ordering drinks is
   1 _____, 2 _____,
   3 _____, 4 _____,
   5 _____.

8. Place the before-dinner drink in front of the guest,
   _____ inches in from the edge of the cloth centered
   between the silverware on a
   _____.

9. Serve cocktails at a table from the _____
   side by balancing tray on left palm.

10. When they are _____ finished, go back to the
    table and offer to refill the cocktails.

11. Suggest a refill by asking
    _____.

12. Coddle them with _____.

13. Be alert either to sell them a fresh _____ or
    to take their _____.

14. Let them make the decision about ordering by asking,
    _____ before I take
    your dinner order?

15. When the food arrives, the beverage is placed between
    the _____ and the _____.

16. At a table all alcoholic beverages are served from the
    _____ side of the guest commencing with the
    first guest to the _____ of the host.

17. For booth or wall table, the correct service is the same
    as that for _____.

18. Ask for _____ of age when
    young persons order alcoholic beverages.

16

The First and Second Course (Appetizers and Salads)

The first and second courses set the tone for a pleasurable dining experience. These courses also enable the guests to watch an expert server at work—you. Attention to detail during these courses will establish your expertise as a server and help your guests to relax and enjoy their dining experience. Guests who enjoy their meal and appreciate excellent service usually tip well.

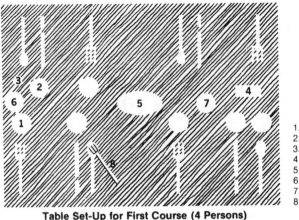

1. Bread and Butter Plate
2. Water Glass
3. Cocktail Glass
4. Bread Basket
5. Relish Tray
6. Sour Cream
7. Butter
8. Cocktail Fork

Table Set-Up for First Course (4 Persons)

1. Place the bread basket (4) and butter in front of the host's bread and butter plate (1), conveniently to his left arm for service to his guests.
2. Place butter (7) as pictured above.
3. Serve the salads to the left of the guest with proper hand. Use underliners for cole slaw, cottage cheese and apple sauce. If the salad is served with the main course, place bowl to the left of the guest, four inches from the edge of the cloth.
4. Shrimp cocktail is served on an underliner and placed in center between knife and fork. Lemon wedge should be on the side of the cup or underliner. Cocktail fork is placed in the bowl of the teaspoon at a 45-degree angle as pictured. Crackers are placed on the underliner. Serve from the left using left hand or booth style.
5. Soup, tomato juice and fruit cup are always served on underliners. Serve from the left using left hand (or booth service). Soup spoon and teaspoon are placed on the right outside of the dinner teaspoon.
6. Remove finished appetizers, empty cocktail glasses, and empty salad bowls.
7. Refill water glasses. Check ash trays. Cover the dirty ash tray with a clean one, remove both ash trays and place a clean ash tray on table.

8. Watch for service number on light board. Check on dinners in case of questionably long delay.
9. Be alert to guests' needs at table you just served and to your other guests.

Review (Chapter 16)
Fill in the blanks with correct answer from this list:
(Answers are contained in Appendix C, pages 225–229)

salad bowls	water glasses	cocktail glasses
prepare	appetizers	lemon wedge
lemon wedge	four	needs
right	salad	

1. Serve the _____ from the left of the guest.
2. A _____ should be on the side of the shrimp cup /or underliner.
3. If salad is served without dressing, garnish it with a _____.
4. Salad bowl is placed _____ inches from the edge of the cloth.
5. Soup spoons are placed to the extreme _____ of the dinner teaspoon.
6. Remove finished _____, empty _____ and empty _____.
7. Refill _____.
8. Be alert to guests' _____ at the table you just served as well as to your other tables.
9. Learn how long it takes to _____ food items.

17

The Art of Super Selling, Taking the Order

Servers must be good sales people because they are selling a product the guest cannot see, touch, smell or taste before purchasing. Restaurant selling is selling merchandise and services sight unseen.

Eighty percent of our guests do not know what they are going to eat until they look at the menu. It's up to you to help them, if they require help, and suggest the extras which make the dinner an unforgettable treat. Remember, people eat out for adventure, not just for good food and good service.

When the average person dines at home, or is a guest in someone's home, he is given little or no choice in the courses that will be served to him. The first thing we require of a guest before we can serve him is that he make a choice from the 70 to 90 items listed on the average menu. This is impossible for the vast majority of our guests, because of the mass of items which tempt him or his lack of knowledge about the products listed on the menu.

You are your guest's guide through the maze of decisions which he must make while selecting his meal. To do this effectively and promptly you must have a plan of sales and carry it through with dispatch to ensure guest satisfaction. Before serving any guests, be sure to study your menu breakdown information. This is what you need to know about each and every item on your menu:

Entrée	Abbreviation	Preparation	Accompaniment	Description	Price
Lobster Tails	LBTL*	Broiled	1. Hot butter 2. Lemon	(2) 6-8 oz. Tails	Market Price

*Some restaurants use numbers for entrée abbreviations. This system is easy to memorize (we use cheat sheets for a while) and much easier for the cooks to read if you don't have a computer.

More About the Dinner Menu

You should have a simple explanation for the meaning of foreign or unfamiliar terms on the menu. Know the contents of the dishes and be prepared to describe them. Any suggestions to help the guest select a meal he will enjoy will ensure his good will in return.

A restaurant should have a description of menu items. Knowledge of the menu is the number one step in being a professional sales person. It will help to make you an expert. Some entrées require extra utensils for the table setting and/or some extra condiments or sauces.

"Suggestion" Selling

The key to "suggestion" selling is to do the thinking for the guest by recommending à la carte items as you lead him through the order.

When the guest is ready to have his order taken, follow the guide (see "The Grid System" page 90) at the top of the guest check: 1. Entrée, 2. Side Dish (list choices), 3. Salad and Salad Dressing (list choices), 4. À La Carte Extras, 5. Beverage, 6. Appetizer (if not sold during cocktail step). Suggest a dish which you know is available at once for the guest who is in a hurry. The procedure for taking the dinner order is as follows: (1) As you look at your guest say, "Ma'am/Sir, are you ready to order?" The presold guest will order immediately. The undecided guest will need your help in making his entrée selection. (2) When suggesting entrees, always recommend one of the best selections from each category: one beef, one seafood, one poultry and one feature of the house, commonly called a signature item, or another favorite.

Write down the number or abbreviation of the main course your guest has selected. Never show personal distaste in his food selection. Everyone's taste is not the same.

If steak is ordered, ask how he would like it prepared: rare ®, medium rare (MR), medium (M), medium well (MW), or well done (WD). "Would you like an order of fresh broiled mushrooms with your steak?" Offer the choice of potato. If you have a house specialty potato, suggest it. Now try to sell an order of French fried onion rings or other à la carte items. Don't offend the guest by overselling. Is the item sufficient for two or more? Inform the guests of this. They appreciate your concern for their welfare. Proceed to the salad and ask his preference for cole slaw or fresh garden salad. If he chooses the garden salad, say "Our house dressing is _____ (describe) or my favorite is _____ (describe)". Pause for a decision. They will give you direction. Never ask,

"What kind of dressing would you like?", because the guest will just have to ask, "What kind do you have?"

Follow through with the beverage by asking, "Which beverage do you prefer?" Eighty percent of guests will have coffee with dinner or later or they may want tea, milk or soft drinks. **Key point!** Always serve cold beverages with dinner. By doing this, you eliminate unnecessary conversation and save yourself time in taking the order.

Next, suggest the appetizer, putting the item you wish to sell last. (The last thing you hear is usually the thing you remember.) Start by asking, "Would you like some fried mozzarella, French onion soup, or a fresh shrimp cocktail?"

Note: The appetizer may also be sold and served after the cocktail order, before taking the dinner order. Always try that approach first.

Take the menu from each guest as you complete their order, unless they are still reading it. Don't snatch the menu away from the guest while he is still reading it. Many guests enjoy looking at the menu. So it should be left with them as long as they're interested in it. As you leave the table smile and thank each one of them as a group. (Let your eyes convey the message.)

Use attractive descriptions when suggesting menu items such as: *chilled* tomato juice, *fresh* shrimp cocktail, *crisp* French fried onion rings, *fresh* broiled mushrooms, *fresh* baked pies. How these words stimulate the appetite and your sales! Try it!

Asking for the Wine Order

Let them know you have wine. Wine service is one of the ancient traditions of hospitality. It gives a restaurant an air of distinction, refinement and showmanship unequaled by any other merchandising methods. If your operation has wine available, use it to increase your guest's pleasure and sense of pride in dining. Immediately after taking the dinner order say, "May I suggest a bottle of _____ or a glass of wine with your dinner?" Listed below are some reliable suggestions for your verbal use:

- Sauterne or Liebfraumilch with white meat and seafood.

- Beaujolais or Burgundy with red meat.

- Rosé is an excellent selection with any dish.

Today, however, it is not unusual for your guests to order a red wine with fish or a white wine with meat. As you receive the order, repeat it verbally and write it down. Know and use your restaurant's standard abbreviations.

One very important aspect of wine service that you should keep in mind is that in addition to lending a touch of elegance to an ordinary meal, there is really no finer or easier way to boost an ordinary check . . . *and along with it your tip!*

The guest who orders cocktails before dinner and orders a steak is more easily sold then the one who orders the lowest-priced dinner and nothing before dinner. Don't be discouraged if you don't always make a sale. The best salesman in any line of business is not the one with the glib tongue, but the one who keeps plugging. We had a server whom we called "Little Annie." She was tops in sales and we asked her the secret of her success. Her reply was, "Use 'suggestion' selling at *every* table."

The Presold Versus The Undecided Guest

The guest you will serve will be either a presold guest or one whose actions indicate that he is confused or undecided.

If your guest is a presold guest, he will make his selection of the main course immediately after being asked. He may then give the server some other parts of his order, or in a few cases may give the server the complete order without help or prompting.

It is our observation that many presold guests look quickly at the menu, order the main course, and hand the menu back to the server. You must then carry him through the rest of the order verbally.

If your guest is undecided you could probably count to 7 without receiving an order, or the count may be interrupted with a statement to show that the guest has turned his meal selection over to you. The most familiar lines are "What's good today?" or "What would you suggest?" Never say, "Everything's good." You're not helping the guest and he is asking for your professional opinion. Follow the suggestions as outlined on the previous page.

À La Carte Orders and Sandwiches

With à la carte orders, one must sell even harder than when the meal is ordered from a table d'hôte menu. To sell extra items you must be positive in your approach.

It is important that you be exceptionally careful when guiding the guest through the meal selection process. A guest must be offered opportunity to select potatoes, salads, beverages and appetizers.

Many sales dollars have been lost by the server being an order taker instead of a salesperson, by failing to inquire if the guest desires other items.

If the guest selects a sandwich and beverage, he has made two choices. It is up to you to encourage him to make other selections by using skillful salesmanship techniques.

Carry him through by asking, "Would you like an order of French fries or French fried onion rings with your sandwich?"

For salad sales, suggest cole slaw or fresh garden salad with all sandwiches. With a steak sandwich, suggest an order of fresh broiled mushrooms or a choice of potato.

We can teach you to sell, but it is up to you to do the selling. There's a world of difference between being an order taker or a super salesperson. It can mean many, many dollars in your pocket over a period of time.

Read this section several times to understand completely the importance of the art of selling. Failure to master the art of selling is the major weakness in the restaurant industry today. Suggesting additional items is not being pushy. You are simply exposing the guest to the wonderful items you have available.

Let's study the following example which proves just how much extra money is made just by using "suggestion" selling.

"Suggestion" Selling:
Here's What's in it for You

Example:

Assuming a 15% gratuity, let's examine the following order for one person—

Order A

An average order with no "suggestion" selling:

Alcoholic Beverage	$ 4.00
Strip Steak	15.00
(Sal & Pot include)	
Coffee	1.00
Dessert	3.50
TOTAL	$ 23.50
Tip (Approx. 15%)	$3.60

Order B

Using "suggestion" selling:

Same order	$23.50
Add:	
2nd Alcoholic Beverage	4.00
Onion Rings	3.00
After Dinner Beverage	3.50
TOTAL	$34.00
Tip (15%)	$5.00
(20% for professional service)	$6.80

In one evening serving six four-tops (24 people) and one six-top (6 people) or 30 guests, note the results below:

30 guests @ $3.60 = $108.00 in TIPS (Example A)

30 guests @ $5.00 = $150.00 in TIPS (Example B)

A difference of $42.00 in one evening by using "suggestion" selling techniques.

If you work four days per week at even a 15 percent TIP, that's $600.00 per week multiplied by 50 weeks. That's *$30,000* versus $21,500 ($432 [example A] multiplied by 50 weeks).

Isn't it smarter to be a salesperson instead of an order taker?

Review (Chapter 17)

Fill in the blanks with correct answers from this list:

(Answers are contained in Appendix C, pages 225–229)

positive	smile	a bottle of wine
carry him through	presold	with bleu cheese
the rest of the	hurry	extras
order verbally	verbally	undecided
steak	thank each of	at the menu
last	distaste	cold drinks
suggestion selling	help	entrée
guide	sale	with dinner or later
eighty percent	confused	two
menu	selling	

1. _____ of our customers don't know that they are going to eat until they look at the _____.

2. It's up to you to _____ if they require help and suggest the _____ which make their dinner an unforgettable treat.

3. You are your guests' _____ through a maze of decisions.

4. Suggest a dish you know is available for the guest in a _____.

5. The undecided guest will need help with his _____ selections.

6. Never show personal _____ in the guest's food selection.

7. If _____ is ordered, ask how it is to be prepared.

8. If they choose garden fresh salad ask, "_____?"

9. With the coffee order ask, "_____?"

10. Serve all _____ with dinner.

11. Immediately after taking the dinner order say, "May I suggest _____ with your dinner?"

12. Put the items you wish to sell _____.

13. As you receive each order, repeat it _____.

14. Many guests enjoy looking _____.

15. As you leave the table, _____ and _____ them.

16. Don't be discouraged if you don't always make a _____.

17. Use _____ at every table.

18. The guest you serve will either be a _____ guest or one whose actions indicate that he is _____ or _____.

19. After the guest has selected his main course and handed the menu back, you must _____ _____.

20. Have ready for him at least _____ items from the menu.

21. To sell extras you must be _____ in your approach.

22. We can teach you to sell, but it is up to you to do the _____.

18

Guest Check Handling—The Check Writing System

Have you ever wondered how some servers remember everything the guest orders? The secret is that they don't rely on their memory. They use what is called the "position system."

The "grid" or "position" system for writing your orders is designed to enable you to serve each guest without ever having to ask, "Who gets what?" You will use one of the systems described below depending on the type of check you have in your operation.

Before working with the following check writing systems, you must first memorize all your abbreviations for the
items on your menu. It is critical that you do not waste valuable time writing out your orders in full. Take a moment to
write out this order: NEW YORK STRIP STEAK, MEDI-
UM RARE, BAKED POTATO WITH SOUR CREAM
AND BUTTER. Now write the same order using these
abbreviations: Str, Stk, BT, MR, BP sc/b. The first time it
took 30 seconds to write the order. Using the abbreviations,
it took only 7 1/2 seconds! That is about 4 times quicker!
Multiply that times the number guests and you've got quite
a bit of time used up that could be much more efficiently
used in serving a second round of cocktails or opening a
second bottle of wine. Remember, steps are time and time is
money, money out of your pocket. If you don't abbreviate
and save that valuable time for something more productive,
you lose money.

Get a list of standard abbreviations from your manager.
Then continue with the next section.

Position System I—This system was designed for the server who can write orders directly on the guest check without
having to consolidate (combine "like" items) for the kitchen.

Position System II—The Grid System was designed for
those servers who must consolidate their orders for the
kitchen. Write the order on a grid first to ensure serving the
right food and beverage to the right guest without asking
who gets what.

Writing the Order

Always write your orders neatly and legibly on the guest
check, using the abbreviations that were given to you. Stand
to the left of the guest with the guest check on your serving
tray. *Never* set your tray or your check on the table in order
to write. It's unprofessional.

Fill out the top of the check completely with: Date, Server, Table Number* (Not section number) and Number of People.

Some guest checks have a grid built right into the check. For those that do not, you will need to carry a small pad and draw your grids on it. Use Position System 1 for your check writing procedures.

The Position System I—Knowing Who Gets What (See page 90)

It is time to take the dinner order after you have established that the guests are ready. Establish eye contact and ask pleasantly, "Are you ready to order?" Or, if cocktails have been ordered add, "Or would you like to relax a little longer and enjoy your cocktails?"

Every order that is written is placed on a certain line or position on your check according to where the guest is sitting. *Always number your guests going clockwise* starting with the pivot point, which is the point where you would naturally approach the table.

At a booth, the first person on your left would be number 1. The person next to the wall on the left is number 2, the person inside on the right would be number 3 and the person on the outside on the right would be number 4.

Again, always start with the person on your left as you approach the table and that person is number 1. Number the remaining guests going clockwise. To remember who is number 1 (for those tables you may approach from a different point each time), you may write some distinguishing characteristic by the first line, for example, red hair or blue sweater.

*Each table should have a number so you can easily differentiate the orders from various tables in your station. This eliminates presenting the wrong check to your guests.

Bar and kitchen orders must be written vertically (up and down)—Line 1, line 2, line 3, etc. Orders for soup, salads, desserts and beverages should be written horizontally across the line to save space on your check.

Whether an order is written up and down or across the line, it must relate to where the guest is sitting. Line 1/Guest 1, Line 2/Guest 2. Examples to follow.

Key Point: If a guest is not ready to order, skip a line or space and go to the next guest. Return to the guest and write his/her order in the space you left open.

Key Point: Use a dash (—) to signify an order of nothing.

Writing the Cocktail Order

Write the cocktail order vertically. Draw a line between orders.

W/W   The guest on your left would get the whiskey and
X MN   water, guest number 2 would get the dry
MOLS   Manhattan, guest number 3 would get the
CHBL   Molsen and guest number 4 the glass of Chablis.

Writing the Appetizer Order

Write the appetizers horizontally at the very top of the guest check.

Use a dash (—) to signify an order of nothing. In other words, if one of guests does not want an appetizer, write a dash (—) where the order would have gone so you know that you asked and when you go to serve the others, you won't serve that person something he didn't order.

Here is an example of a "horizontal" order using the position system for the appetizer order:

A-CHK / — — — / MZR/ PT SK

Guest number 1 ordered artichoke hearts romano, number 2 ordered nothing, number 3 ordered mozzarella fingers and number 4 ordered potato skins.

Whether you write the order going up and down or across the line, you still use the *Position System* and put the order in the proper sequence on your guest check according to the seating arrangements of the guests. The first order goes on the first line, the second order on the second line. Or, in the case of writing the Appetizer, the first order goes on the first space, the next order to the right of the previous one, etc.

Go to the computer and punch your order in.

Writing the Soup and Salad Orders

Write the soup order horizontally along a line to save space for the entrée orders. The salad order should go on the next line. A typical order may look like this:

MNS / BF

FRD / OVD / O & V

MNS = Minestrone Soup
Bf = Beef Vegetable
FRD = French Dressing
O & V = Oil and Vinegar

Writing the Entrée Order

Draw a line after the appetizer and soup and salad orders have been written.

Write the entrée order vertically on the check. Each entrée must be on a separate line with a side dish selection to the right of the order. *Bring special items or requests to the attention of the cooks by highlighting it.*

Write the entrée first then the side to it on the same line. If there are two sides, write the second one below the first and go to the next line for the next entrée. See sample on the next page.

Write temperatures for all steaks cooked to order using the proper abbreviation (R, MR, M, MW or W) and *circle* the *doneness.*

An entrée order should look like this:

V Prm / Sp
  GB
Stp M / BP sc, b
  GB
Filet R / MP w G
  GB
  side Msh
V Pct / BP pl
  no veg

Guest number 1 ordered: Veal Parmesan, and side orders of Spaghetti and Green Beans.

Guest number 2 ordered: Strip Steak cooked Medium, and side orders of Baked Potato with sour cream and butter and green beans.

Guest number 3 ordered: Filet cooked Rare, and side orders of Mashed Potatoes with Gravy, Green Beans and a side order of Sautéed Mushrooms.

Guest number 4 ordered: Veal Picatta and side orders of Baked Potato, plain and no vegetable.

Writing the Beverage Order

The beverage order is written on the bottom of the guest check. Leave room for the dessert order. A beverage order should look like this:

c-w / c-l / mlk / c-w

Guest number 1 wants coffee with his meal, number 2 wants coffee after dinner, number 3 wants milk with his dinner and number 4 wants her coffee with her meal.

Note: All cold beverages such as iced tea, soft drinks, and milk are served with the dinners. If there is any doubt, simply ask the guest what he would prefer.

Writing the Dessert Order

The dessert order is written on the grid. Use either the across (horizontal) or up and down (vertical) method to record orders. An order should look like this:

— / choc chs / — / rs ck

Guest number 1 wants no dessert, number 2 wants the double chocolate cheesecake, number 3 wants nothing and number 4 wants the walnut raisin layer cake.

The Position System II— The Grid System

The purpose of the Grid System is also to ensure that you serve the proper person his food or beverage without ever having to ask, "Who gets what?" Follow the same rules for check writing as previously described. However, do all your initial writing using the grid form.

Why use a grid? Often you will be asked to consolidate your orders before turning your check in to the kitchen. This means that you must combine like items to make it easier for the cooks to prepare the items. They want all the strip steaks listed together, all the veal parmesan together, all the baked potatoes together, and so forth. But in doing this for the kitchen, you would have no way of remembering which guest ordered which food unless you first write your order on a grid. The grid is simply a tool to use to keep the orders separated on different lines. Each guest's order goes on a different line.

This is an example of a grid:

	COCKTL	APPET	ENTREE	POT	VEG	EXTRA	SALAD	BEV	DESSRT
1.									
2.									
3.									
4.									

When taking an order, use the top of the check or a grid on a note pad in this order which is the order in which it will be taken:

1. Cocktails (If not written on back of check)
2. Appetizers
3. Entrée or main course
4. Potato
5. Vegetable
6. Extras (such as garlic bread or sautéed mushrooms)
7. Salad dressing
8. Beverage
9. Dessert

Refer to the grid when ordering from the kitchen and setting up your tray. Refer to the grid when serving so you will know who gets what. That is part of being a professional, isn't it?

This is what our order from the previous examples would look like written on the Grid:

	COCKTL*	APPET	ENTREE	POT	VEG	EXTRA	SALAD	BEV	DESSRT
1.	w/w	a-chok	v parm	sp	gb	—	it	c-w	—
2.	x man tw	——	stp m	bp/sb	gb	——	fr	c-l	ches
3.	mols	mozz	filet r	mp/g	gb	mush	fr	mlk	——
4.	chab	pz sk	v pct	bp/pl	——	——	o & v	c-w	rs ck

*When writing repeat cocktail orders, simply put a slash mark or a plus 1 after the cocktail to indicate "one more" like this: w/w +1.

In the above example, and having numbered your guests going clockwise (remember, the first person on your left as you approach the table is number one), you find the order for guest number one on the first line, the order for the next guest on the second line, and so forth.

Now you will have to bring down the order for the cooks on the main part of the check. The top of the check, then, is just for you. It enables you to know who gets what. The bottom part of the check is for the cooks to read to prepare the order.

Separate Checks and Large Parties— Keeping the Orders Straight!

Don't hesitate to ask if there is any doubt as to whether to provide a group with one or separate checks. This is especially true at lunch. Separate checks is the trend. Be sure to ask, "Will this be all on one check?" during the welcome step of your service.

The position systems and the use of a grid can also be a simple means of handling separate checks and orders for large parties where at least two servers are needed.

For a large group, say a party of 16, number the guests going clockwise. One server will take care of guests 1-8 and the other will take the orders for guests 9-16. Number the grid to match the guests. Use the grid and transfer items to a master check. This would mean that two servers working one table would turn in one master check and each makes out her own separate grid.

Has a guest ever said to you, "The lady in red is with me. Put ours together, please." Do you panic? Why, no! You simply draw a connecting line on your grid from his (#3) to her (#7) order. At the end, just copy those orders on their check.

Tip: When making change on separate checks, it is helpful to denote the amount tendered on each individual check on the back, upper left corner. This process will help simplify the cash handling procedure and could eliminate confusion.

The Use of A Master Check

You may be required to write a master check for orders that will later be separated. This is also a simple process when you use the Position System for your check writing.

1. Simply transfer the items on the master check to the separate checks along with the price of the items. Cross off or put a small check mark on the master check as you do,

so that all items are accounted for. Total the items on the mast, check and balance against the total on the separate checks. Do the totals correspond?

2. The use of computers makes handling separate checks simple, accurate and speedy.
3. Add sales tax to separate checks.
4. Write "Thank you" across the check along with your name.

Review (Chapter 18)
Fill in the blanks with correct answer from this list:
(Answers are contained in Appendix C, pages 225–229)

what	eye contact	enjoy
position system	grid	who
tray	pivot point	table number
horizontally	ready	steps
guests	number	server
line	Position system I	relax
date	memorize	money
four	vertically	pleasantly
abbreviations	left	server
space	clockwise	number
left	Position system II	
dash	check	

1. Servers use what is called the _____ to help them remember who gets what.
2. It is important to _____ all your abbreviations for the items on your menu.
3. By abbreviating you can take the order _____ times faster.
4. _____ are time and time is _____.
5. If you write your orders directly on you guest check use _____.

6. If you consolidate your order use
_____. This is also called the
_____ system.
7. When writing the order, stand to the _____ of
the guest.
8. Never set your _____ or your _____ on
the table.
9. Fill out the top of the check with _____,
_____, _____, and
_____ or people.
10. The position system tells you _____ gets
_____.
11. Establish that _____ are ready to order.
12. Establish _____ and ask, _____,
"Are you _____ to order?"
13. If cocktails have been ordered, add, "Would you like to
_____ a little longer and _____
your cocktails?"
14. Always number your guests going _____
starting with the _____ of the first guest on
your _____.
15. In Position system I, bar and kitchen orders must be
written _____.
16. If a guest is not ready to order, skip a
_____ or _____.
17. Use a _____ to signify an order of nothing.
18. Fill in the headings on the grid for a table of four.

1.								
2.								
3.								
4.								

Vegetable   salad   appetizer   entrée
dessert   potato   cocktail   beverage   extra

19

Setting Up—Step By Step

A. Setting up Your Tray for the Appetizer Course

　1. After ordering appetizers from the proper (hot/cold) station, gather required underliners and accompaniments, for example, underliners and spoon for soups, lemon and cocktail fork for shrimp cocktail. Crackers are often served with this first course.

B. Setting up Your Tray for the Bread and Salad Course

　1. Refer to your grid to ensure proper tray set up.

　　a. Reach for tray at same time.

　2. Count out the number of bread and butter plates needed, remembering that you will need extra for butter, appetizers and salads.

　　a. Stack underliners on tray so that heaviest part of weight will be concentrated on your shoulder or in the middle, depending on how you carry your tray.

b. Reach for items in this order: Salads, butter, cocktail forks, crackers.

c. Check salads for appearance.

3. Get a hot butter for following types of dinners if your restaurant serves them: surf and turf, lobster tails and scampis.

a. Place butter warmer on tray along with hot butter.

4. Pick up bread and bread basket last. This ensures hot bread for your table.

5. Set up above could be a guide. Check with your manager as to how he (or she) would like setting up to be done.

C. **When to "Turn In" the Order . . . Timing is the Most Difficult Step in Food Service.**

1. Learn how long it takes to prepare food items.

a. Analyze your menu. Are your items to be broiled, fried or are they from the steam table?

b. How busy is it? Slow, moderate or very busy? Adjust.

c. Check to see how busy the chef is: many orders ahead, or is he/she caught up?

2. Use common sense.

a. A well done steak will take longer than beef from the carving station.

b. Some cooks are faster than others in preparing orders. Know who is working behind the stove.

3. If business is slow, complete your tray set-up before putting in the entrée order.

4. If the restaurant is extremely busy, check spindle for number of orders ahead of you. If there is a backlog of checks, put your order in immediately unless it is a steam table item. In that case set up your tray first.

5. If you are uncertain how to proceed, check with your manager or a more experienced server.

Review (Chapter 19)
Fill in blanks with correct answer from this list:
(Answers are contained in Appendix C, pages 225–229)

sour cream	butter	salads
menu	manager	relish tray
relish tray	steak well done	timing
surf & turf	cole slaw	check
hot bread	appetizers	
lobster	before	

1. _____ is the most difficult step in food service.
2. Analyze your _____.
3. A _____ will take longer than beef from the carving table.
4. If business is slow, complete your tray set up _____ putting in your order.
5. If uncertain about your order, check with your _____ or a more experienced waitress.
6. Refer to your _____ to insure proper tray set up.
7. Extra underliners will be needed for _____, _____, _____, and _____.
8. Check _____ and _____ for appearance.
9. Put crushed ice on _____.
10. Get hot butter for the following dinners: _____, _____.
11. Pick up the _____ last.

20

Wine Service—
A Nice Extra

The bottle presentation is an important part of the wine service and should not be overlooked. When a guest orders a bottle of wine, it should be brought to the table and presented to the host's right side, label up, for his inspection. The bottle should not be wrapped in a napkin. Before presenting the bottle, make sure it is wiped clean. Wipe with a damp cloth if necessary. After the host has approved the wine, the cork is removed.

To open a bottle of still wine —
1. Cut and remove the metal capsule just below the bulge to be found on all wine bottles.
    Put capsule in your pocket.
2. Insert a corkscrew into the cork, holding the bottle in the left hand (not on the table) and extract the cork with the right. Move back from the table (a moment) when the cork is withdrawn to prevent spillage.
3. Wipe the top and neck of the bottle again to remove any bits of cork or dust.

To open round topped bottles, such as champagne or sparkling burgundy—
1. Unwind and remove the wire which holds the cork. (Refer to instructions.)
2. Holding the bottle firmly with the left hand at a 45 degree angle, grasp the cork with the right hand firmly so it will not fly out. Twisting the bottle (not the cork) ease out the cork. Hold the open bottle at a 45 degree angle for a few moments to prevent excessive foaming.

   Caution: warm champagne and/or shaking could cause excessive foaming.

   Always point the bottle directly away from the guest.
3. The napkin should be placed on the side of or across the top of the champagne bucket. The napkin should be used to wipe dripping of champagne or wine.

Wine Table Service

Place wine glass on the table as shown at right. The glass in front of the host is then filled one-fourth full, just enough for a taste. (If the host does not understand why this is done, lean down and quietly ask him to taste the wine. He will catch on quickly.) He will give you a sign that the wine meets with his approval and this will be your cue to serve the guests. Hold the lower one-third of the bottle so that the guest may see and read the label easily. Then serve clock-wise, beginning with the first guest on the host's left and continuing until the host has

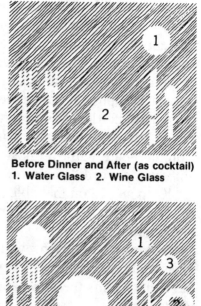

Before Dinner and After (as cocktail)
1. Water Glass   2. Wine Glass

With Dinner.   1. Water Glass
2. Cup and Saucer   3. Wine Glass

been served again. Fill the wine glasses two-thirds full as this allows the wine to breathe. When pouring, as the glass is filled to the proper amount, lift the mouth and turn your wrist clockwise to eliminate dripping wine on the guest or on the table. Use napkin to wipe drips.

If food has been placed in front of the guest and the wine is served with the meal, all wine glasses are placed between the water glass and coffee cup.

After completing the above, all flat wine bottles (those not charged) are placed upright on the table (red wine) or in a wine basket behind the host's wine glass (white or rosé).

Charged (champagne, sparkling burgundy, sparkling red) white and rosé wines are served chilled and placed in an ice-packed bucket (with about 1 cup of water) to the right of the host's elbow, not on the table. The exposed part of the bottle is wrapped with a napkin which acts as a handle grip for the host or server. When additional serving of wine is made, this prevents the wet bottle from slipping in the server's hand. An extra napkin should be folded over the handles of the bucket. You will always have a dry napkin to wipe the bottle and prevent dripping at the table.

A half bottle of wine will serve two, a full bottle will serve four comfortably or five or six scant glasses. Communicate with the host. Is a second bottle needed? Do not use the word "another."

Keep an eye on the table and replenish the guests' glasses. Ask for a reorder, "Would you like a fresh bottle of (use the brand name)?"

Note: When serving white wine, bring the bottle to the glass on the table. Do not lift the glass in your hand because the hand warms the glass and spoils the effect of the chilled white wine.

Serve red table wines at room temperature or slightly cooler—65 degrees. They go well with roasts, cheese and meat dishes, in fact, with all foods except seafood. Not that red wine with fish will do you any harm, it is just that with fish you will enjoy white wine more than red. Rosé wine is fine with either meat, fish or fowl.

Both red and white wines may be kept for a few days (even a week) after opening if they are promptly recorked. Keep recorked white wine in the refrigerator and red wine in a cool place.

Should a guest select a wine which is not available, choose two wines of the same type from the wine cellar. Say, (in a warm, professional manner) "I'm sorry, we're out of _____. May I suggest the _____ or the _____?"

Remember food will sell itself, it's up to you to sell the wine.

In order to sell the wines on your wine list, you must learn about them by studying a *Wine Breakdown Form*. An example of one follows. Have your wine representative or manager complete this outline using wines on your wine list.

In some restaurants, the bin number designates its place in the wine cellar. However, when the bin number is not needed for that purpose, we suggest using the numbers to denote the following, that is, Bin No. 174. The first number stands for type: 1=white, 2=red, 3=rosé, 4=sparkling. The second number for dryness (1) to sweetness (9): 1=very dry, 9=very sweet. The third number can denote the storage shelf.

Bin	Wine	Pronunciation	Red, White, Rosé	Dry — Sweet (1-9)
174	Johannesberg Riesling	Yohonizberg Reezling	White	7

Steps in Opening a Wine Bottle

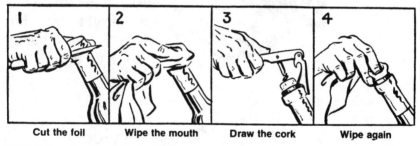

| Cut the foil | Wipe the mouth | Draw the cork | Wipe again |

(Well below the lip of the bottle)

Opening Champagne is a Little Different . . .

Remove top of foil cap, then the wire hood. Hold your finger on the cork so it will not pop out too soon.

Slant the bottle and be sure to point it away from your guest. Grasp the cork firmly. Twist the bottle, not the cork, slowly in one direction. Let internal pressure help push out the cork.

Hold on to the cork as it leaves the bottle. A slanted bottle will not overflow as readily as an upright one, but have a glass handy just in case.

Wine By the Glass Service

Many restaurants stock many house of jug wines that are served in a carafe. Bring the glasses to the table with the filled carafe on your cocktail tray. Set the glasses in their place on the table. Pour the wine from the carafe into the glass. Never pour the wine while the glasses are still on your tray. This would be quite dangerous and difficult.

Review (Chapter 20)
Fill in the blanks with answers from this list:
(Answers are contained in Appendix C, pages 225–229)

turn	label	firmly
basket	right	cork
lift	red meat	either
table	4	breathe
you	bottle	coffee cup
fish or chicken	type	2
white or rosé	charged	suggest
2	$^1/4$ holding left	water glass
corkscrew	$^2/3$	clockwise
elbow	wine glass	
flat	we're out of this	

1. The wine that is ordered should be brought to the
   _____ and presented to host's _____ side
   _____ up for his inspection.
2. When opening a bottle of champagne, hold the bottle
   _____ with the left hand and the
   _____ firmly with the right hand.
3. Twist the _____ and not the cork.
4. Insert the _____ into the cork
   _____ the bottle in the left hand and
   extracting the cork with the right.
5. All _____ bottles are placed on the table or in
   a wine _____ behind the host's _____.
6. _____ wines are placed in an ice bucket,
   to the right of the host's _____.
7. A half bottle with serve _____, a full bottle will serve
   approximately _____.
8. The glass in front of the host is filled _____ full.
9. Serve _____ beginning with the first guest
   on the host's _____.

10. Fill the wine glasses _____ full as with allows the wine to _____.
11. When pouring, as the glass is filled with the proper amount, _____ the mouth and _____ your wrist toward you.
12. Wine served with the meal is placed between the _____ and the _____.
13. Check to see if the _____ wine is chilled.
14. Rule of thumb: white wines with _____; red wines with _____, rosé with _____.
15. If the selection is not available, choose _____ wines of the same _____ and bring them to the table.
16. Say, "I'm sorry, _____. May I _____ . . . ?"
17. Food will sell itself, it's up to _____ to sell the wine.

21

Dinner Plate Inspection (Picking Up)

In the kitchen be sure to inspect the plates before you serve them. Ask yourself these questions:

1. Is it your order?
2. Is it hot?
3. Is your order correct?
4. Is your order complete?
5. Is it properly prepared?
6. Is it the right quantity for serving?
7. Is it attractive and properly garnished? Does it have eye appeal?
8. Is the plate free from spilled food on the edges?
9. Do you have all the food and necessary serving pieces for the courses on your tray?

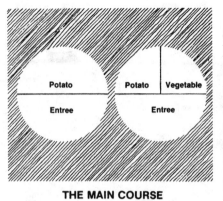

THE MAIN COURSE

Guests react to color just as they react to taste. Plate layout and presentation are an important part of your work. The most common mistake made in plate presentation is that the vegetable and entrée are positioned improperly before the guest. It is important that the entrée always be placed directly in front of the guest.

Examine the orders carefully as you collect them in the kitchen. A good company philosophy is, "If you're not proud of it, don't serve it." Accept only those orders that are right. Check for appearance, garnishing and quantity. If any item does not meet with your approval, have it replaced. Refer the matter to the kitchen supervisor. Learn the correct garnishing so that nothing will be forgotten during the rush hours.

Side dishes should be used only for those vegetables which are served in a juice or sauce, such as stewed tomatoes. Other vegetables could be placed on the plate in an attractive manner. These procedures are established by management. Do not use your own discretion.

When side dishes are used for vegetables and potatoes, they are positioned above the plate with the potato side dish to the guest's left and the vegetable dish to the right of the potato.

22

Dinner Service Sequence

1. If you're not proud of it, don't serve it.
2. When serving dinners, serve those that are most apt to get cold first, such as roast beef, lobster, and scampi. Steaks served on hot platters and deep fried foods will stay hot. If a plate is hot, be sure to warn the guest.
3. The main entrée items should always be placed directly in front of the guest.
4. Check to see if anyone ordering steak has a steak knife.
5. In serving meat with a bone, the bone should be to the back. This allows the guest to make the first cut directly into the meat.
6. Place French fried onion rings in the center of the table if they were ordered to be shared.
7. When serving steak, ask at that time, "Would you please cut your steak in the middle so I'll be sure that it's done

the way you like." Inquire as to which steak sauce they prefer. Serve that one only (personalized service.)

8. Steak sauces should be served with the caps on to allow the guest to shake the sauce. Catsup may be served with the cap off. Be sure the bottles and tops are clean.

9. Eighty percent of people have catsup with the French fries. Serve it automatically.

10. Remove any unnecessary glassware and dishes. Change ash trays if necessary. Refill water glasses.

11. Check table to see if more bread and butter are required.

12. Serve beverages to those who have them with their dinner. Work with your head and not your back. Save steps.

13. Check back within one minute or two to three bites, whichever comes first, on dinners. Ask, "Are your dinners prepared the way you like?" Then, "Is there anything else I can get for you?" **Key Point**—Guests appreciate this point of service. If there is a problem and you resolve it immediately, that is the end of it. However, if you are not there to fill that need, the guest could become quite aggravated. I cannot emphasize enough the importance of this step. *Check back with your guests one minute after serving.*

14. Don't ask "How are your steaks?" This could imply poor quality.

15. If guests are satisfied they will let you know. If they are dissatisfied with the way a steak is done, offer to return it to the kitchen for additional broiling or replace it if overdone.

16. If a guest makes a complaint regarding food which you serve him, ask his preference for another item and make a report of it immediately to your supervisor. Check your house policy on handling complaints. If the guest doesn't complain, but doesn't eat, say (with genuine interest) "I notice you're not eating your dinner." Pause and wait for a reply. Do not ask if anything is wrong with his dinner. The guest will let you know if there is.

17. Acknowledge the fact that you will be there for further service if they need you.
18. When a guest leaves a large portion, suggest, "May I box it for you?"
19. Remove the main plate when each guest in a party is finished. If they put their silverware on the plate, that's usually a sign they want you to remove it. Remove all accessory (side dish) plates only when all guests are finished. Remove bread and butter plate last. This does not apply at tables where guests arrive at different times. Keep each guest in his own order of service unless ordered to do otherwise.
20. All that now should remain on the table are water glasses, cups and saucers, teaspoons and napkins.
21. Serve coffee. Be alert to offer coffee to those who did not order it during the meal. Refill water glasses. Change ash trays by capping them with a clean one. Place the clean ash tray on the table.

Review (Chapters 21 and 22)
Fill in the blanks with correct answers from this list:
(Answers are contained in Appendix C, pages 225–229)

bread	hot	hot
water glasses	warn	spilled
back	done the way you	serving
on	like?	steak
correct	Proud	coffee cups
bread and butter	garnished	main plate
plate	prepared	in front of a guest
now	box	How is your steak?
butter	ash trays	Prepared cold
French fries	first	side dish
serve	your order	teaspoons
complete	catsup	

1. About your order: first, is it _____?
2. Is it _____?
3. Is your order _____, _____
   and properly _____?
4. Is it the right quantity for _____?
5. Is it attractive and properly _____?
6. Is the plate free from _____ food on the edge?
7. If your not _____ of it, don't
   _____ it.
8. Serve those dinners _____ that are apt to
   get _____.
9. If a plate is _____, be sure to
   _____ the guest.
10. The main course item is always placed
    _____.
11. The bone should be to the _____.
12. Check to see if every has a _____ knife, if
    necessary.

13. Steak sauce should be served with cap _____.
14. Always ask if they would like _____ with their _____.
15. Change _____ when necessary.
16. Check table to see if more _____ and _____ is required.
17. Ask if the steak is _____. Don't say, "_____?"
18. Ask, "Are your dinners _____ the way you like?"
19. If there is a problem, _____ is the time to deal with it.
20. When a guest leaves a large portion, suggest, May I _____ it for you?
21. Remove the _____ when each guest in a party is finished.
22. Remove _____ last.
23. All that should remain on the table after the main course is completed are the _____, _____ and _____ and napkins.

23

Non-Alcoholic Beverages

In American restaurants non-alcoholic beverages include tea, coffee, milk, iced tea, milk shakes and soft drinks. All non-alcoholic beverages are served from the right side of the guest, starting with the first guest on the left side of the host and continuing in a clockwise manner. Remove empty glasses from the right side with the right hand. When tea is served, whether hot or cold, serve a slice of lemon. All cold beverages are served with the dinner.

When non-alcoholic beverages are served with the meal, they are placed to the right of the guest and to the right of the silverware, four inches in from the edge of the cloth. This four-inch position is the most convenient spot for a guest to raise the glass or cup while eating. The cup handle is placed at a 45-degree angle, so it requires no wrist action or turning of the cup in raising it to the lips.

Pots containing additional portions of the beverage served during the meal are placed above the cup or glass. Cream and sugar for the coffee and tea are then placed next to the pot. Serve all beverages by the base only, never with fingers on the drinking edge.

Coffee

When coffee is requested with dinner, it is brought to the table immediately after the entrées have been served. Cups, saucers and cream should be brought from the kitchen when you bring out the dinners. Set the tray on the stand, serve the dinners and then place cups and saucers to the right of the guest. Go to the service station to get a pot of coffee and a

Don't forget 20 after 12 for cup handle

liner. **Note:** Always carry the pot in your hand to avoid splashing guest. Carry a shield (bread and butter plate) in your free hand. Do not carry a coffee pot on a tray; this is very dangerous.

Procedure for serving coffee after dinner:
1. Stack saucers in center of small round tray.
2. Fill cups at urn with the handles facing out.
3. Work off round tray at table.
4. Place coffee cup on saucer by using thumb and first finger in handle (never on lip of cup!)
5. Pick up off tray by saucer. Serve to right of guest with handle at 20 after 12.

The procedure for four or more is the same, but use a square tray. When the coffee pot is on the tray stand, it should be in the center of the tray to avoid accidents.

When booth service is used, the coffee container is carried to the table with a small underliner. The underliner is placed down on the end of the booth. The coffee container is then grasped in the left hand and the coffee cups on the right side of the booth are filled in the same order as food service is made. When cups on the side of the booth are filled, the coffee container is placed down on the underliner and the handle is switched to the right hand. Coffee service is then made to the left side of the booth. Practice this for a while. You will see how much more gracious it is.

Be alert for coffee in the saucer. Replace with clean saucer or remove the cup and saucer, clean and return them to the table. A paper coaster to absorb spilled coffee is a good idea.

A great little idea of guest awareness is serving the left handed person's coffee from the left side with the left hand so you won't have your elbow in guest's face. Do you know how to tell they are left handed? They eat with their left hand. Correct?

Refilling Beverages

Refilling beverages served at the table is an art. It should not be undertaken without a considerable amount of practice.

A cup or glass *should not be raised* from the table once it has been positioned. All second refills are done by following this rule: *Pour to the table.* Don't pick it up! The reasons for this rule are two-fold: (1) It is safer—less handling and (2) It is more efficient—one step, not three. The coffee or water is then poured into the cup or glass from the container held in the right hand. This really gives the restaurant class.

For convenience, a refill pot of coffee could be brought to the table on an underliner. The handle of the container is grasped by the right hand. The underliner is placed under the pot with the left hand supporting it. Upon reaching the table, the underliner should be dropped away and held in the left hand.

The underliner should then be placed between the guest and the cup to prevent splashing and shield steam. If the thermal pot is to be left on the table, an underliner should be placed under it for your convenience as a shield for next pouring. If you are busy, the guest can pour his own, but it is much nicer if you refill—the personal touch!

Pour water to glass on table

Protect guests from splashing

Don't pick up cup or glass

24

Selling the Dessert and After-Dinner Beverages

Dessert sales are easy. Many servers make the error of confusing the guest by not giving him a clear picture of what the restaurant has to offer in the way of desserts. The question "Would you care for dessert?" does not give a clear picture of what pleasures can be expected from the dessert service. As a result, most guests simply take the easy road out by saying, "No, I don't care for any."

To sell desserts, you must draw a word picture of the desserts offered for the guest. You must assume that he will make a choice if he is offered a limited selection. Be positive in your approach and follow these rules:

1. After clearing the table and refilling coffee, explain, "For dessert this evening we have apple crumb pie, blueberry cobbler, chocolate mousse, fresh strawberry pie and one of my favorites—a pecan ball—which is vanilla ice cream rolled in chopped pecans with warm butterscotch topping."
2. Look at the first guest and ask, "Sir, would like to try the strawberry pie or the pecan ball?"
3. Continue to offer dessert to each guest. "Ma'am, which would you prefer?" Suggest sharing dessert with another guest if one guest says s/he is too full.

How to Serve the Dessert

Pick up your dessert order. Set up your tray with proper silverware.

Place the silverware down first on the right of your guest.

Place the dessert plate in the center with the left hand (or booth service). The point of the pie always faces the edge of the table.

Note dessert fork on right

The fork is always on the right in serving dessert.

Every restaurant operator should increase the showmanship aspect of his operation. Showmanship automatically increases the prestige and excitement elements available to his guest. The individual server likes to make a good show of his/her services.

One of the simplest, least expensive and easiest forms of showmanship, from the standpoint of training, is platter service. This will be used in presenting all of the desserts on the tray. How can the guest refuse? When using this concept, never ask the guests if they would like to see the dessert tray; simply bring it after clearing their entrée course.

After-Dinner Beverages

Don't forget to also offer an after-dinner beverage for the dessert course. Often they are more welcome by the guest than a heavier dessert. Actually, they are quicker to get, and also a higher price than desserts (up goes your tip!) Say, "May I suggest a Bailey's Irish Cream or a Kahluah and coffee?" The procedure for after-dinner cocktails is the same as for dessert. Put cocktails on a bar tray with the correct number of cocktail napkins in your fingers. Serve on the right hand side of the guest with the right hand.

Always be alert to pour additional coffee during the dessert and after-dinner course.

Change ash trays (don't forget capping). Refill water by filling glasses on the table.

Review (Chapters 23 and 24)
Fill in the blanks with correct answers from this list:
(Answers are contained in Appendix C, pages 225–229)

fresh	dry	saucer
underliner	right	left
saucer	lemon wedge	Bailey's Irish Cream
Kahluah & Coffee	two	right
coffee	fresh	table
pour	base	word picture
cold	center	positive
drinking	after dinner drink	20 after 12
edge wipe	right	

1. _____ beverages are served with dinner.
2. Beverages are served from the _____ with the _____ hand.
3. Serve all beverages by the _____, never with fingers on the _____.
4. Handles are placed at the _____ position.
5. An _____ is used as a shield in pouring coffee.
6. Place coffee on table by lifting the _____.
7. Be alert for coffee in the _____. Replace or _____.
8. Rule for refilling is _____ to the _____.
9. Always serve a _____ with iced or hot tea.
10. To sell desserts you must draw a _____ of the desserts offered.
11. Be _____ and pre-select _____ tempting desserts.

12. If the fruit is _____, be sure to say _____ in your description.
13. The dessert plate is placed in the _____ with the _____ hand.
14. The fork is always placed on the _____ in dessert service.
15. If dessert isn't ordered, suggest an _____.
16. Two popular after-dinner drinks are _____ and _____.
17. Be alert to pour additional _____ during dessert course.

25

Presenting the Guest Check

When to Present the Check

At breakfast the check should be presented when the guest is finishing his main course and his coffee or other beverage has been replenished. At lunch the check is presented when the guest has been served his dessert and his coffee or other beverage has been refilled. At dinner the check is presented when the guest has finished his dessert and his coffee or other beverage has been refilled. In those restaurants which serve alcoholic beverages, the check is presented after the guest has finished ordering.

Don't keep a guest waiting for the check! This is just before determining the tip and the last impression of the restaurant. You have run the race and you must cross the finish line. Do not irritate the guest now!

Presentation Procedure

1. Recheck the top of your check to correspond with the bottom if using the grid.
2. Be sure your name and table number are on the check.
3. Be sure of prices and double check.
4. If the table does not order dessert or an after-dinner beverage and has indicated no more beverages, then total your check away from the table and present the check on a tip tray.
5. When dessert is ordered and after it is served, refill coffee, total check away from the table and present it.
6. If an after-dinner beverage is ordered and consumed, return to table for a second sale. If none is ordered, you may then present the check.
7. How the check is handled is just as important as your greeting. The check is the guest's finished product of his transaction with you. It must be clean, neat, readable and correct.

Don't forget to smile

Follow These Rules for Guest Satisfaction

1. Never lay your pad on the table to write or total your checks.
2. Always total your checks away from the table.
3. Many restaurants with computers put the check in a hard cover booklet or on a tip tray.
4. Write "thank you" and your name on the check. Psychologically this increases tip percentages.
5. Low-key the check presentation—do not hold it in the air.
6. Present check face down on the tip tray or plate to the right of the host or in the middle of the table if the host is unknown.
7. Say, "Thank you. It was a pleasure serving you." SMILE!
8. Explain the payment procedure. Say, "Whenever you're ready, I'll be happy to take this up for you."
9. If they don't offer to pay the check at this time (which they ordinarily do), leave the table and continue with the service to your other tables.
10. Be alert, take nothing for granted. The guest may change his mind and want another cocktail or more coffee.
11. As soon as you see he has placed the money or charge card on the tray, ask, "May I take this for you?" Repeat amount tendered, "Out of $50, sir."
12. Take the payment to the cashier stand. At the register, repeat amount of money given to cashier and count the change.
13. Coins should be on top of bills, with large denominations on the bottom.
14. Place the tip tray down gently to the right of the guest who paid, hesitate, make eye contact, smile and say, "Thank you, it's been a pleasure serving you and come back again soon!"
15. It is not necessary to count the change back to the customer.
16. Be sure the tip tray you present is spotless.

17. Wait until the guests have left to claim your tip.
18. If a guest has placed his money or credit card on the tip tray and the server serving the party is at the bar or kitchen, don't keep the guest waiting. Take the money or card to the cashier's stand. She should do the same for you. Teamwork!

Handling Charge Accounts

1. The guest will usually place the credit card on the tip tray. You will be exposed to American Express, Diners, Master Charge, Visa and perhaps your own restaurant's credit card. Many operations will have the servers handle the check paying procedures.
2. Select the correct form and place card in machine. Transfer card information onto the form and guest check. Make sure all charge information is legible.
3. Date, fill in the amount on both forms and the back of the guest check. Leave gratuity open. Remove credit card from machine. Get approval code if over limit and card is declined. Return to guest and say politely (and quietly) "We're having a problem with our machine, do you have another card we could try?"
4. Return to table. This is the perfect opportunity to see the guest's name on his charge and use it. Say, "Thank you, Mr. Jones. Would you sign this for me, please?" (That's a professional service technique.) The guest will now sign and fill in the gratuity if it is not going to be a cash tip. *Never stand over a guest while s/he is signing the charge and calculating your tip.* Walk away or monitor the table so you will be available when s/he signs the charge.
5. If it is your restaurant's charge, he will fill in the back of the check himself. If not, copy name, address, credit card number and amount. Be sure to check credit card number index at the cash register, if you have one. If not, this may be a good idea to incorporate into your operation.

6. Be certain writing is legible. If not, politely ask for his card number or name and print it on check.

Skip Artists

There is always that very tiny minority of guests who will use your facilities and buy your firm's products and services with no intention of paying for them. If you work in a restaurant where you are responsible for all your checks, the skip artist or deadbeat is stealing from you. But even if the house takes the loss, you can help by observing whether the guest stops to pay his check on the way out. It is best to take care of checks for the guest.

Some people who wish to charge a check to a house account just naturally sign their names in such a way that they are impossible to read. Many of these are steady guests who just assume that everyone at the restaurant, even new staff members, knows who they are. But some skip artists use this as part of their technique. While not everyone who signs a check with an unreadable signature is a skip artist, you should see to it that any checks you take to the cashier for a house charge have a readable signature as well as an address for billing purposes. Maybe have a stamp that says "Print your name" and "Please sign here."

Lost payments, whether by accident or design, come out of profits. Check your restaurant's policy as to who suffers the loss. But whether it's you or your boss, take steps to reduce skips to the absolute minimum.

Exercise extreme tact in talking to anyone who "forgot" to pay his check or uses an illegible signature. The one thing you don't want to do is insult a good customer.

Review (Chapter 25)
Fill in the blanks with the correct answer from the list:
(Answers are contained in Appendix C, pages 225–229)

Master Charge	finished ordering	May I take this for
repeat	table number	you
top	coffee	on the table
3/4	prices	away
coffee	alert charge	name
American Express	Diners	legible
granted	top	Visa
dessert	waiting	correct
spotless	main course	refill
bottom	Thank you	
tip tray	coins	

1. At breakfast the check is presented when the guest has finished his _____ and his_____ has been replenished.
2. At lunch, the check is presented when the guest has finished his _____ and his _____ has been refilled.
3. In restaurants serving alcoholic beverages, the check is presented after the guest has _____ and acknowledged he is ready for his check.
4. When _____ of the after-dinner beverage is consumed, return to the table for a _____ or a second sale.
5. Recheck the _____ of the check to correspond with the _____.
6. Put your _____ and _____ on all the checks.
7. Be sure to double check _____.
8. Never lay your pad _____ to write or total check.

9. Total check _____ from table.
10. Take nothing for _____! Be _____!
11. As soon as you see he has placed his money on the try ask "_____?"
12. _____ amount of money given to cashier and count change.
13. _____ should be on _____ of bills.
14. Place the _____ down gently, _____ and say "_____ come back again."
15. Be sure the tip tray you present is _____.
16. The check must be _____ and _____.
17. Don't keep the guest _____ for his check.
18. The credit cards in general use are _____, _____, _____, _____.
19. Make sure all _____ information is legible.

26

Don't Forget the Children

When families go out to dinner, the first thing they consider is—where do the kids want to go? Very few restaurants cater to families. If you want this type of business, here is what to do.

Pay special attention to the children. Many parents are in a state of tension, fearing what Timmy will do when he eats out. Do your best to bring small children their food quickly. It will save both them and their parents much anguish.

McGarvey's has a national and Ohio state award-winning menu for children eight years old and under. Be sure the children have a menu and crayons. This keeps them entertained. Bibs should be given to very small children only. Suggest to parents that tying a knot in the corner of a cloth napkin and tucking it under the neck line will also take the place of a bib. Ask the parent if the tiny tot or baby would like crackers to keep him satisfied until the meal is served.

If the parents have a cocktail before dinner, serve the children a kiddie cocktail (cherry juice, 7-Up and a cherry with a short straw in a small glass.) This is another way to make the kids a part of the show.

McGarvey's kiddie menu consists of bunny salad, entrée, snowman sundae and milk. Kiddie cups are used for milk or soft drinks. Small glasses are suggested. They are easier for the kids to handle.

When the server brings a snowman sundae to the table, s/he also brings a toy. This is another McGarvey way of living up to our motto—"We love kids!" (Write for an award winning kiddie menu.)

Don't forget the children

Editor's Note:

Ed Solomon was a national award winner for his family promotion in a merchandising contest sponsored by The Pepsi Cola Co. and The National Restaurant Association.

His children's menu won 1st prize in Ohio and his unique young adult menu won 1st prize on the national level. For any additional information on how to promote family business call (216) 926–2608 in Grafton, Ohio and ask for Ed or Shelly.

27

Little Tricks of the Trade

The "Buddy System"—Be a Team Player

Ask your co-worker, "Do you need anything?" This improves guest satisfaction, saves steps, and makes an easier work load. It is just as easy to pour coffee and water for the guests of your co-workers when you are pouring for your own station. Help your buddy and she'll help you in return.

Save Steps

Did you know it takes at least 12 trips to one table for an average meal? The experienced server will work tables as one by co-ordinating the orders.

137

Example:

1. Table 12 may be on dessert.
2. Table 13 may need cocktails.
3. Table 14 may be ready for the first course.

If possible, bring as many of these items as you can to your station and several tables in one trip. Your service will be faster and you will have saved yourself time and trips. Through the use of time and study, the experienced server may be able to cut down the trips from 36 to 24 or less. Faster turnover, better service, less fatigue! What a combination! (See also Chapter 12).

Do Not Go Empty Handed!

Pick up items you may need at your station or service area if you are not carrying trays in and out of the kitchen. Another step saver.

Pre-set large tables with bread and butter plates, water and coffee cups. Saves time.

What's the Difference?

When serving more than one look alike cocktail, use a different color swizzle stick to designate the difference. Example: Vodka and gin martinis: Use a different color pick for olive. Perhaps red for vodka and green for gin.

What's Left?

Only a small percentage of our population is left-handed, but they never fail to be impressed if you serve their coffee on the left. In this instance, the coffee handle should be at 20 minutes to 12. Do you know how to tell if the person is left-handed? They usually eat their dinner with their left hand! I have talked to many left-handed people and they all say that servers are not aware of the fact that they are left-handed. Being aware is another sign of a true professional.

28

"Selling" Your Restaurant

The Personal Touch

The guest, the absolute essential in the operation of the business, is a self-willed individual who will not usually patronize a business unless he is satisfied with the service. The business life of a restaurant depends upon a clientele of happy, satisfied guests.

To establish and keep the good will of the guest, a favorable image must be maintained which is created by both the physical aspects of the operation and the guest-employee relationships.

The most effective way for the guest to be informed is through you.

Courtesy to Our Guests

1. Be alert for extra service. Watch for signs of birthday, anniversary or other celebrations.
2. Offer to get cigarettes and cigars. Bring them to the table and open the pack for them. Light their cigarettes.
3. If the guest asks a question you cannot answer, refer to the supervisor or someone who can help you.
4. If baked goods may be bought to take out, explain this to the guest.

Light those cigarettes

Promotions

Has management let you know about "house features"? Here are some ideas that could be used.

1. **Banquet Facilities**—If the guest inquires about party facilities, inform the manager or supervisor.

2. **Special Parties**—Promote wine tastings, a night in Italy, gourmet dinners, or other such theme parties.

3. **Holiday Celebrations**—Easter, Mother's Day, Thanksgiving, Valentine's Day.

4. **Special Menu Features** such as buffets. Use menu clip-ons and table tents to help promote features.

5. **Catered Parties**

6. **Wedding Receptions.**

7. **Advertising**—Sales persons should be familiar with and put into practice the different kinds of advertising. 86 percent of your first time guests come because of word of mouth, according to the National Restaurant Association.

8. **Reservations.**

9. **Hours of Operation**

"The Willingness to Serve is Just as Important as the Service Itself."

Questions Patrons May Ask . . . Can You Supply The Answers?

Just as the concierge answers questions for the hotel guests, so might you be asked to help your guests with answers to the following questions:

Facts

1. What is the local population?

   _____

2. Why was this town so named ?

   _____

   _____

   _____

3. For what is this town noted ?

   _____

   _____

   _____

4. Give names of colleges or schools in town.

   _____

   _____

   _____

Entertainment

1. Names of special points of interest

   _____

   _____

   _____

2. Where is the nearest and best public golf course ?

   _____

   _____

   _____

3. What place is best for swimming ?

   _____

   _____

   _____

4. What movies are playing at the leading movie houses and when ?

1._____

_____

2._____

_____

3._____

_____

Locations

1. Name of leading department store?

_____

2. Name of leading furniture store?

_____

3. Name of leading jewelry store?

_____

4. Name of leading men's store?

_____

5. Name of leading women's store?

_____

6. Name of leading drug store?

_____

7. Where is the Post Office?

_____

8. How can I get to the turnpike?

_____

9. Which is the best route to the airport?

_____

_____

_____

10. Where is the bus station?

_____

_____

_____

Review (Chapters 26, 27 and 28)
Fill in the blanks with correct answers from the list:
(Answers are contained in Appendix C, pages 225–229)

empty handed	steps	easier work
buddy	special attention	service
colored stirrer	one	satisfied
feed	patronize	birthdays
favorable	supervisor	service
twelve	left	serve
kiddie cocktail	anniversaries	crackers
cigarettes	you	good will
kitchen	small glasses	the parent

1. Pay _____ to
   the children.
2. Bring _____ quickly to small
   children.
3. _____ are
   served when mom and dad are having cocktails.
4. Ask _____ if the tiny tot
   would like _____ to keep him satisfied.
5. _____ should be used for
   milk or soft drinks.
6. The guest will not _____ a
   business unless he is _____ with the service.
7. To establish _____ a
   _____ image must be maintained.
8. If the guest asks a question you cannot answer, refer it
   to the _____.
9. Be alert for extra _____.
10. Watch for signs of _____,
    _____ or other celebrations.
11. The most effective way for the guest to be informed is
    through _____.

12. Offer to get cigars and _____.
13. The willingness to _____ is just as important as the _____ itself.
14. The "buddy" system saves _____ and makes an _____ load.
15. Help your _____ and she'll help you in return.
16. A server should work her tables as _____ by co-ordinating her orders.
17. It takes at least _____ trips to one table for and average meal.
18. Do not go _____ in or out of the _____.
19. When serving more than one type of mixer, use a different _____.
20. Southpaws will be impressed when you place their coffee on the _____ with handle at 20 minutes to 12.

29

Banquets and Parties

1. Check with the supervisor or party book for details.
   A. How many?
   B. Head table? Table arrangement? Microphone?
   C. Main course? Steak knife? Hot butter? Steak sauce?
   D. Appetizer?
2. Drape head table (optional).
3. Set up individual setting as pictured. Allow a minimum of 24 inches per person (30 preferably). Guest comfort (no squeeze please) is of prime importance.
4. Bread basket and knives, one per six persons.
5. Ash trays, one per four persons.
6. Salt, pepper, and sugar, a set per six persons.
7. Butter and sour cream, one per four on underliners with serving spoon on side.
8. Creamer, one dish per six persons.

9. Dressing tray, one per ten (if used).
10. Table decorations as ordered.
11. Banquet sections should be assigned to each server by the supervisor to begin serving up appetizers and salads. Warm appetizers and salads will start the party off on the "wrong foot."
13. Serve appetizer. Clear.
14. Serve salads.
15. Serve bread (preferably warm).
16. Pick up empty salad bowls and cocktail glasses.
17. Serve main course.
18. Pour coffee, other beverages as requested. Pour to the table! Do not pick up the cup.
19. Refill water glasses. Pour to the table! Do not pick up the glass. Speeds up service and less chance of accident.
20. Change ash trays.
21. Do not remove main course plates from your assigned table until the main course has been cleared from the head table.
22. Clear all tables of everything except coffee cups, saucers, teaspoons and water glasses.
23. Serve dessert to the head table, then to the other tables.
24. Refill coffee and water, clean ash trays.
25. If the banquet has a program which is about to start, leave the room unless requested to stay to serve after-dinner drinks.
26. Follow all the rules of table service. Food from left, beverages from right. Remove to a tray from the same side.

Review (Chapter 29)
Fill in the blanks with correct answers from the list:
(Answers are contained in Appendix C, pages 225–229)

main course plates	head table	cups and saucers
coffee	appetizer	water glasses
salads	24	main course
head table	rules	water glasses
after-dinner	ash trays	coffee
appetizer	salads	timing
supervisor	cocktail glasses	
water	ash trays	

1. Check with _____ or party book for details.
2. Allow _____ inches per person.
3. On parties, _____ is of utmost importance.
4. The procedure for serving parties is serve _____, _____ and bread and butter.
5. Pick up finished _____, _____, and empty _____.
6. Use all _____ of table service.
7. After serving the main course, pour _____, refill _____.
8. Change _____.
9. Do not remove _____ from your assigned table until the _____ has been cleared from the _____.

10. Clear all tables of everything except
_____, teaspoons and
_____.

11. Serve dessert, _____ first.

12. Refill _____ and
_____. Change _____.

13. Leave room unless requested to serve
_____ drinks.

30

Tableside Service

The purpose of this chapter is to suggest some modern techniques that will enable servers to learn their tasks more efficiently without sacrificing the grand or flamboyant manner required for effective tableside cookery.

Much of this chapter was taken from a book called *The Essentials of Tableside Cookery* by Durocher & Goodman. Write Cornell Hotel and Restaurant School, 327 Statler Hall, Cornell University, Ithaca, New York 14853, c/o Joan Livingston, Associate Editor.

Tableside service is variously referred to as "French," "Russian," and "cart service." The distinguishing feature of this style of service is that there is some form of preparation of various dishes simplified by three means:

1. Preportionment of component ingredients in the kitchen which saves valuable time in the dining room.
2. The use of pre-tested, carefully specified procedures for describing task units.
3. The use of standardized recipes.

By streamlining the tableside presentations in the above fashion, patrons are hence allowed to enjoy personalized attention without waiting inordinate lengths of time for their food.

By using the above techniques, a server with only minimal training can present a well-prepared product to the patron only five minutes from the time tableside preparation is begun.

Tableside service can be used to lend variety and merchandising appeal and to contribute to the guest's satisfaction.

Equipment Needed (available through your equipment dealer):

A tableside service cart with hinged leaves and one or two undershelves.

A réchaud or flaming lamp—with LP gas preferably for faster cooking. Some flaming units use clean burning fuel (canned gas) while others use denatured alcohol. The clean burning fuels leave no carbon deposits on cooking utensils and are especially desirable when producing flaming coffees.

Supplies Needed for Tableside Cooking:

Sauté pans, crêpe pans, sauce pans, condiment holders, carving equipment, serving utensils, serving platters.

Steak Diane
(serves one)

Preparation and Service
Equipment Needed:
Tableside service cart—side leaves up
Tablecloth (to cover top of cart)
Réchaud—with gas flame
12″ to 14″ stainless steel pan
Utensils—two dinner forks, two large serving spoons
Cloth napkins

Recipe:

Item	Amount
Strip Steak (defatted)	6 to 8 oz.
Butter	3 tablespoons
Salt	Pinch salt
Pepper (fresh ground)	
Cognac	1 oz.
Chopped Shallots (finely chopped)	2 tablespoons
Worcestershire Sauce	1 tablespoon
Whole Garlic	1 clove (minced)

Cooking Method:
1. Melt butter, add finely chopped shallots and cook until shallots are lightly browned. Add all other ingredients (except cognac). When it begins to brown, add steak and cook for three minutes. Turn and cook for two to three minutes or until done to taste. Add one oz. cognac. Tip pan to catch flame and then tip pan back. Flame will burn out in a matter of seconds.
2. Transfer to serving dish and sprinkle touch of salt and small amount of freshly ground pepper.
3. Pour sauce over steak.

Bon Appétit!

31

Better Safety Than Sorrow

1. Clean spills immediately. If possible, throw a napkin or cloth on the spill if you have to walk away.
2. Be sure trays are secure and balanced on stands.
3. Do not overload on one side of tray so it will be upset. Turn all cup handles in toward center of tray.
4. Watch for other employees. If you are approaching from behind, warn them by saying, "Behind you."
5. If glasses or dishes are broken, cover and have them removed at once.
6. Watch for broken or chipped china or cracked glass which should be discarded.
7. Be careful going through swinging doors. Observe in and out rules.
8. If you see a fire, report it quietly. Know the location of fire extinguishers.

9. Check chairs and tables for broken parts, splinters and rough edges. Report to manager.
10. Be alert for spilled water and foods on floor. Good shoes will prevent slipping on any surface.
11. Report all injuries to your supervisor, describing how it took place. File a report.
12. Know where the first aid kit is kept.
13. Do not over lift. Ask for help. When lifting heavy trays, keep back straight and use your leg muscles.
14. Walk, do not run.
15. Remember, haste makes waste!
16. Be careful not to cross path of fellow workers or bump into them.

32

Incentive Program

Many restaurants have sales contests and usually the same two or three servers win consistently. With our type of sales program, everybody's a winner. The house makes money, the servers get a commission, and the guest enjoys an adventure in dining.

McGarvey's uses a unique sales incentive program. It might not be applicable to every restaurant, but we like it and our servers like it.

Very simply, it rewards servers with extra income for the extra items they sell. For example: if servers sell appetizers, French fried onion rings, fresh broiled mushrooms, or other à la carte items which help boost the amount of the check, pay them five to 10 cents per item depending on the gross profit of the item(s).

While some state liquor laws prohibit the use of incentives on sale of alcoholic beverages, if your state permits it, it is a good idea to have incentives for every alcoholic beverage first round, and on wine by the glass or bottle. We suggest 10 cents for every beverage after the first round. Twenty-five cents to a dollar per bottle of wine based on the selling price.

It does not take very long for those extra nickels to add up to extra dollars in the servers' pockets and the boss' pocket, too. So teach servers to use "suggestion" selling.

It is imperative that the results are posted where everyone can see them.

The number one want of employees is recognition. The incentive program is ongoing and the results are measurable.

It also makes management aware of who needs additional training when you have a few who are not performing up to your standards. Professional training is imperative. Follow the service scenarios (either alcoholic or nonalcoholic) for teaching the procedures step by step with our new alcohol service scenario.

Seventy-six per cent of your guests tip a percentage of the check. Twelve per cent tip the same amount all the time and twelve per cent don't believe in tipping at all.

The higher the check usually means a better tip, but *only if the service is professional.*

Another Incentive Idea

Another commonly used incentive program is to calculate guest check average (sales divided by customer count) and post it weekly, monthly and at year's end. The server(s) with the highest guest check average wins recognition and monetary rewards. Be sure to *post* results!

33

Procedure for Bussing Tables

The name bus boy comes from the Latin word *omnibus,* meaning many things at the same time. The job covers many, many tasks and is very important. A busser's primary responsibility is the cleaning and resetting of tables after the guests have gone. Other jobs may include assisting guests and waiters, and maintaining cleanliness and order in the dining room and kitchen.

Appearance is of the utmost importance. Hair should be clean, neat, short and out of eyes. Clothing should be clean and pressed. Shoes should be well polished and well fitted. Personal cleanliness is a must.

Bus personnel should be well mannered, polite and cheerful. "Please" and "Thank you" should be used in guest and fellow employee relationships. Even though it is the servers' job to serve the guest, many times you will be called on to fulfill a guest's need when the server is busy. It might be serving water or refilling coffee. Practice pouring to the table. You should acknowledge the guest with a warm smile and a cheery, "Hello."

A fast, efficient busperson can increase the turnover in the restaurant. Many servers tip buspersons for helping and it is just smart business for doing your best because it is an important thing in the ladder of life.

As you reach the table, push all the chairs in, so you can reach across the table easily.

Take all remaining silverware off the table first, using both hands. Do not pick silverware up with one hand and put it in the other. Place silverware on outer edge of tray in the same direction. This makes it easier for the dishwashers to handle the silver to be washed. Handle by the handles only, never by the eating end.

Move the glasses together and you can pick up four at one time—not with your fingers, but by the bases. Coffee cups and saucers are next, Stack the cups together (two or three in a stack). Be aware of coffee left in cups so it does not spill. Stack the saucers and remove. Place these items on your tray with the heaviest items on your tray to one side. Be sure your hand and shoulder will support the bulk of the weight. Silver along the side and cups, saucers and glasses in the center. Keep all like items together.

Or, you may put the heaviest weight in the center and cups, saucers, silver and glasses to the side. The key point is to balance the tray so it doesn't tip and cause a crash in the dining room.

Dump the ashtray and other refuse on the placemat (if used). Twist the placemats so nothing will spill out. Collect napkins and place them on tray.

Always use a tray or bus tub when bussing to save time and steps.

Duties On the Floor

1. It is the primary duty of a bus boy or girl to keep the tables clear and to move the soiled dishes to the kitchen.
2. As soon the guest leaves, clear, clean and reset the table for the next party.
3. You may be assigned to a certain section or work wherever needed. When not cleaning tables, be alert to guest needs. If the server is too busy:
   A. Fill water glasses
   B. Refill coffee cups
   C. Empty ash trays by capping the dirty one with a clean one and place the clean ash tray on table.
   D. Keep service stations stocked with items needed.
4. Do not brush crumbs on floor or chairs. With a damp cloth, brush crumbs to edge of table and pick up with cloth or brush. Wipe tables with damp towel. Check chairs for cleanliness. Wipe chairs with a different colored dry cloth and scoop into your hand if there are crumbs.
5. Be alert for paper or food particles on the floor. Sweep up around chairs where small children have been sitting. Use silent butler and small broom.
6. Wipe off high chairs and junior chairs with a damp cloth before returning them to designated area.
7. Stack trays properly and carry to kitchen.
8. Bring back needed supplies and a tray for future use.

Duties Off the Floor

1. Keep cups, saucers, glasses, ice and silverware stocked.
2. Make coffee if the servers are too busy.
3. Stock paper supplies and food supplies such as coffee and tea.
4. Pick up empty trays and racks and store in proper place.

The key to maximum efficiency . . . Don't go in or out of the kitchen empty-handed. Bring in soiled trays or empty racks. Carry out supplies as needed. Check with food checker on way out for food orders ready to be served and carry out to server.

Duties at Closing

1. Wipe down all tables.
2. Assist servers with side work and tear down tray stands.
3. Restock all dining room supplies as needed for the next day. Check with supervisor for any further instructions before leaving.

Note: Several of our bussers have graduated to server positions. Their practical on-the-job training helped them considerably in learning procedures and methods of proper guest service.

Review (Chapter 33)
Fill in the blanks with correct answer from this list.
(Answers are contained in Appendix C, pages 225–229)

cleared	alert	empty-handed soiled
stocked	stock	supplies
tray	in	glasses
turnover	reach	bulk
both	hand	other
direction	out	shoulder
saucers	tray	4
support	cups	stop
tip	balance	
time	appearance	
omnibus	crumbs	

1. The name busboy comes from the Latin word
   _____.
2. _____ is of utmost importance.
3. It is your primary duty to keep tables _____
   by removing _____ dishes.
4. When not cleaning tables be _____
   to guest's needs.
5. Keep service stations _____ with
   items needed.
6. Don't brush _____ crumbs onto floor or chairs.
7. _____ trays properly and carry
   to kitchen.
8. Bring back needed _____ and a
   _____ for future use.
9. Don't go _____ or _____ of the
   kitchen _____.
10. A fast efficient busperson can increase
    _____.
11. Push all the chairs in so you can
    _____ across the table.
12. Take silverware off the table using _____ hands.
13. Don't pick up silverware with one _____
    and put in _____.
14. Place silverware on _____ in same
    _____.
15. Move the _____ together so you
    can pick up _____ at a time, by the bases.
16. Stack _____ together. Stack _____
    separately and remove.
17. Be sure your hand and _____ will
    _____ the _____ of the weight.
18. Key point is _____ the tray so it
    doesn't _____
19. This is a _____ saving and
    _____ saving method of bussing tables.

34

The Dining Room Host/Hostess— Supervisor or "Super Vision"

Personal Appearance and Attitude

The dining room host-hostess/supervisor is usually responsible to the manager. S/he may be in charge of the dining room area. This means the room itself and all those who work in it. Many restaurants prefer a supervisor who has had experience as a server and, therefore, understands the service problems and has knowledge of the work involved.

The supervisor is the key to a successful operation in the dining room. His/her attitude toward the guest is reflected in all service personnel under his/her supervision. *A supervisor's prime concern is guest satisfaction.*

The first 30 seconds are very important in guest satisfaction. The guest's first impression of your restaurant can affect his appetite. The cheerful "hello" from the hosts and hostesses will do much to make him feel welcome.

He/she must have a neat appearance, pleasant expression, friendly smile and possess a well modulated speaking voice. Tact and good judgment are especially beneficial for someone in this position.

S/he must be willing to assume responsibility and to handle constructive comments. The host-hostess should be impartial in rendering service to the guest and in attempting to handle guest complaints.

The motto of a good dining room supervisor might be, "Be alert and take nothing for granted." Follow through on assignments and be alert to guest needs by observing the dining area. Instill in the service personnel the importance of satisfying the guest, attempting to see that he goes out praising the fine food, excellent service and warm reception he has received.

Co-workers must be treated on a fair and equal basis. Friendliness, not over-familiarity, should be encouraged. S/he must keep their cool under trying circumstances. As s/he doles out constructive comments (in private), s/he should also give praise when it is earned (in public). And remember, it is always better to be a leader than a driver.

Responsibilities of a Host-Hostess/Supervisor

1. Supervise food service employees and inspect their appearance.
2. Assign dining room stations and make sure all sidework duties are carried out.
3. Check reservation book for table set-ups and required personnel.
4. Be prudent in minimizing the costs of operating the dining room.
5. Maintain a check list before the serving period.

   Example:

   Supplies: If low, have bus person replenish. If depleted, make out a requisition.

   Service stands: Completely stacked with the required items.

   Menus: Complete? Clean? Dog-eared?

   Side work: Assigned and completed?

   Dining room: Neat? Clean? Tables and chairs clean? Windows and draperies? Light bulbs needed?

   Kitchen: Features of the day? Low or Out items? Posted?

6. Have your dining room station plan set so that you know exactly where you are going to seat your guests as they enter the dining room. Plan ahead! A turn sheet should be kept to record number of people, not number of tables, given to each server. Keep in mind that even though the turn system is used, the customer service area should be kept as close together as possible. Do not have the server working both "sides" of the dining room or s/he will be taking too many steps and too much time to serve her/his guests.
7. Be sure service personnel are on floor at required time and have received any special instructions.

Key Points in Receiving Guests

1. Stand near the entrance to the dining room and greet guests with a smile. "Good evening, Mr. Smith." (Use a name if you know it.) "Are there four in your party?" Try to be alert as to the number. If you cannot determine at a glance, then say, "Good evening, how many in your party?" If there is a single, never say, "only one?" The best thing to say is "Good evening, sir. Nice to have you with us," and then escort the guest to the table. Make the guest feel important.

2. Ask if you may hang their coats or assist with packages.

3. Don't walk too rapidly!

4. Seat elderly and handicapped guests near the entrance so they will not have to walk too far.

5. Try to apportion the seating so that each serving station has an equal amount and the waitress is not overloaded. Avoid seating two tables in one station at the same time whenever possible. Never triple-seat!

6. Pull out the chair for a woman guest if she is alone or if the man does not assist her.

7. Place the opened menu before each guest and tell them the name of their server.

8. Check the table at a glance for clean ash trays, clean silverware and napkins.

9. Provide a booster chair for small children and a high chair for babies. It is a good idea to have a special menu and crayons to keep the children busy while waiting for their food.

10. Be sure that the table you are taking the guests to is cleared of soiled dishes and has been reset. Never seat guests at a dirty table. If a guest requests a table that is not ready, have them wait by the hostess' area.

11. Alert the server to her new guests and inform her if they have any special requests regarding a special occasion or the check presentation.

12. Continually study work stations of servers so you will know where the next guests can be seated.

Overseeing the Service

A hostess' job does not end with the seating. It is her duty to see that the guests' orders are taken without delay and they are served correctly. Again she must use her "super vision."

1. If the waitress is detained in taking an order, the hostess should be ready to take it or direct another person to do so. Bring water and perhaps take a cocktail order.
2. Watch the service at various tables. Be sure the water glasses are filled, ash trays clean, butter, sour cream and coffee refilled when necessary. Get the message to the server: "Coddle the guest with kindness." We suggest using table numbers when referring to tables in the dining room.
3. By keeping the server aware of guest needs you ease the work load on them and yourself. It becomes—a habit. Criticize the server in private; praise in public.
4. Know how to apply "suggestion" selling and be sure the servers apply it while taking the order.
5. Watch the food served. It should be up to your restaurant's standards, both portion-wise and quality-wise. Inquire tactfully about the quality of the food and service. "I hope you are enjoying your dinner. Is there anything I can get for you?"
6. Have bussers clear and reset the tables promptly. The trays should be removed from the dining area as soon as the table is cleared.

There are times when the supervisor must handle complaints and deal with difficult guests. Keep in mind that 90 percent of the problems can be solved if the server gets back to the table within the first minute after serving and asks, "Is your dinner (lunch) prepared the way you like?" Always be sincere and attentive. Express your regret at any of his complaints and try to rectify them! Remember! The guest is not always right, but he is never wrong! First. Listen to the complaint and don't interrupt. Use the words, "I don't blame you for being angry, what can I do to solve the problem?"* Don't say, "I know how you feel," because that could infuriate them even more.

When guests are leaving the restaurant, instead of asking, "How was everything?"*, say instead, "We hope you enjoyed your evening. Please come back soon."

You may sometimes be requested to relieve the cashier, operate the paging system and answer telephones. When taking reservations, get all desired information and write it in the reservation book. A reservation idea that has worked successfully is to assign code letters and numbers to anyone making a reservation. Whoever takes the reservation uses his initials for the code letter and the number of guests for the number. For example: if the hostess Kathy Peterson takes a reservation for the Johnson party of 12, she gives the code KP12. The advantage is that if there is an error or omission, you know who made it or if the guest says (on a busy night), I have a reservation and it's not written down, you can ask for a code which verifies whether or not they really did have a reservation.

*If there was a problem it should be solved at the table by the server.

Closing Duties

1. It is the supervisor's job to see to it that all personnel in the dining room have a break. They must report to him/her when leaving the floor.
2. Before the bussers leave, check to see if they have stocked and put away equipment.
3. Before each server leaves, *inspect* . . . don't expect that closing duties have been performed.
4. Reinforce positive work ethics—give them the pat on the back! It costs nothing and means much.

Review (Chapter 34)
Fill in the blanks with correct answer from list.
(Answers are contained in Appendix C, pages 225–229)

server	be alert	important
30	"suggestion" selling	super vision
entrance	public	single diner
host-hostess/	customer	equal basis
supervisor	satisfaction	smile
ahead	assign	private
fair	granted	overloaded
apportion	kindness	
one	equal	

1. The _____ is the key to successful operation in the dining room.
2. Coddle the customer with _____.
3. Co-workers must be treated on a fair and _____.
4. Plan _____.
5. Be alert and take nothing for _____.

6. Alert the _____ to her new
   quests and inform her if they have any special requests
   regarding special occasion or the check presentation.
7. Try to apportion the seating so that each server has an
   _____ amount.
8. If there is a _____ never
   say, "only one?".
9. Stand near the _____ to the dining
   room.
10. _____ and take nothing for granted.
11. Criticize the server in _____,
    never in public.
12. If there is a single, never say, "Only _____?".
13. Try to _____ the seating.
14. Co-workers must be treated on a _____
    and equal basis.
15. _____ dining room service stations.
16. The hostess' prime concern is
    _____.
17. Try to apportion the seating so that each serving station
    has an equal amount and the server isn't
    _____.
18. Make the guest feel _____.
19. Greet the guest with a _____.
20. Praise the server in _____.
21. Know how to apply _____.
22. The first _____ seconds when guest enters
    the restaurant, are very important in guest satisfaction.
23. A hostess must use her _____.

35

Restaurant Jargon

Restaurants have their own language. Many words are derived from or are foreign words. We have listed some of them.

À La: After the manner or in style of.

À La Broche: Cooked on a skewer.

À La Carte: By the bill of fare; each item having a separate price.

À La Florentine: served with spinach.

À La Goldenrod: Chopped, hard cooked egg whites in cream sauce. Grated yolks as a garnish.

À La King: Cooked in a cream sauce, with pimento or green pepper, mushrooms, etc.

À La Mode: In cooking: served with ice cream: a. side of pie. b. Braised with vegetables and served in a rich gravy.

Ambrosia: Cold dessert of bananas, shredded coconut and oranges.

Anchovy: Small fish, used in olives and canapés and in Caesar salad.

Antipasto: A course of smoked or salted meat, fish, vegetables, etc., served as an appetizer.

Aspic: Any jellied dish or gravy.

Baba Au Rhum: Round cake soaked in rum.

Bain-Marie: A steam table or double boiler.

Baked Alaska: Ice cream on cake, covered with meringue and browned.

Bavarian Cream: Gelatin and whipped cream.

Béarnaise: A sauce made with eggs, butter, shallots, tarragon and lemon.

Béchamel: A rich white sauce with spices, usually made with cream.

Bisque: A cream usually of shellfish or chicken. Also frozen dessert with nuts.

Bill of Fare: A list of dishes provided at a meal: menu.

Bon Appétit: A good appetite to you.

Booster Chair: Child's chair made to fit on a standard chair.

Bordelaise: A brown sauce containing celery, carrots, onions, thyme, butter and bay leaves.

Borsch: Russian soup made of beef stock, beets, tomatoes, seasoning, and sour cream.

Bouillabaisse: Fish soup; five or six varieties of fish and shell fish simmered together. White wine is added before serving.

Bouquet Garni: Bouquet of herbs tied together to facilitate removal after use. Usually parsley, marjoram, chervil, tarragon, thyme, bay leaves.

Brie Cheese: Soft cheese from Brie, France. Often served warm with French bread and fresh fruit.

Brochettes: A small spit used in roasting; skewer.

Broth: Liquid in which meat has been cooked.

Brunswick stew: Veal or chicken cooked with corn, onion, tomatoes, potatoes, etc.

Brut: unsweetened, natural, raw.

Buffet: 1. A sideboard for china, glassware, etc. 2. A counter for serving meals or refreshments, or a restaurant with such a counter. 3. A meal at which the guests serve themselves.

Butter Warmer: Container holding candle or alcohol to keep melted butter hot.

Caesar Salad: Salad consisting of romaine lettuce in a dressing of olive oil, anchovies, lemon juice, vinegar, Worcestershire sauce, mustard and egg. Sprinkled with parmesan cheese and black pepper. Tossed with fried croutons.

Café Noir: Clear black coffee.

Camembert: Soft full-flavored cheese; served as or with dessert.

Canapé: An appetizer made of fried or toasted bread spread with anchovies or other savory foods.

Carafe: Glass bottle for wine or other liquids.

Carte Du Jour: Menu of the day.

Casserole: A fireproof dish in which food is cooked.

Charlotte Russe: Sponge cake or split lady fingers with sweet flavored whipped cream and gelatin.

Chartreuse: Any combination of chopped foods in a mold.

Chateaubriand: Thick tenderloin served surrounded by duchess potatoes and a variety of vegetables.

Chafing Dish: A vessel with a heating apparatus beneath it, to cook or keep food warm at the table.

Chef: Head cook.

Chive: Diced slender onion tops.

Chiffonade: Served with shredded vegetables.

Chutney: A relish of fruit or vegetables.

Clarified Butter: Pure melted butter.

Cobbler: Deep dish fruit dessert with biscuit topping.

Cocktail: An appetizer; may be juices, fruit, shellfish, or alcoholic beverage.

Cocktail Fork: Very small fork.

Compote: 1. Fruit stewed or preserved in syrup. 2. A dish for holding fruits, etc.

Condiments: Spicy high-flavored seasonings used as relish, such as mustard, catsup, etc.

Consommé: A light colored clear soup made of meat stock.

Coquille: Shell. En Coquille—in or on a shell or ramekin.

Coupe: An ice cream dessert.

Creole Sauce: Sauce prepared with green peppers, tomatoes and onions.

Crêpe Suzette: Thin egg pancake usually served aflame in cognac or curaçao.

Crêpes: Thin pancakes.

Croquettes: Mixture of chopped and cooked foods, shaped and rolled in egg and bread crumbs and deep fried.

Croutons: Small pieces of bread crust toasted and sautéed.

Cuisine: Style or quality of cooking.

Curry: From India; a highly spiced powder used in seasoning.

Demitasse: Small cup of strong black coffee served without cream or sugar at the end of the meal.

Decanter: A slender-necked glass bottle into which wine is poured for use at the table.

Deuce: A table for two.

Deviled: Highly seasoned, chopped and mixed.

Drawn Butter: Melted butter. Drawn Butter Sauce: Butter, flour and salt.

Dupe: Short for duplicate. Used in referring to tickets turned in for extra items.

Éclair: A small oblong pastry, like a cream puff, filled with custard or whipped cream and icing.

Eighty-Six—"86": As in "86-Board" in kitchen, listing what you're out of that day.

En Coquille: Cooked in the shell.

Entrée: the principal course at a meal.

Escargots: snails.

Filet: A boneless loin cut.

Filet Mignon: Tenderloin of beef often wrapped in bacon.

Finger Bowl: Small bowl containing warm water, usually served with a towel and lemon, for cleansing the fingers.

Flambé: Served with flaming brandy or other liquor.

Fondue de Fromage: A melted cheese dish.

Frappé: Partially frozen; iced.

Fricassee: Poultry or veal cut into pieces, stewed and served with gravy made of stock and milk.

Garnish: 1. To add something to by way of decoration; embellish. 2. In cookery, to decorate (a dish) with flavorsome or colorful trimmings.

Glacé: Anything that is iced or frozen, or anything having a smooth glossy surface attained with meat glaze, sauce, jelly or sugar.

Goulash: Beef stew simmered with paprika or other seasonings; usually served with noodles.

Gourmet: Person who is discriminating in what he eats and drinks.

Gratin: Au Gratin: Fish, meat or vegetables, baked in oven until golden brown. Usually includes bread crumbs.

Gratuity: A gift usually of money given in return for services rendered; tip.

Grenadine: Syrup of pomegranates or red currants used in various mixed drinks.

Gumbo: Soup made of meat, okra (a must), tomatoes, green peppers and seasoning.

Hollandaise Sauce: Made with egg yolk, butter and lemon juice.

Hors d'oeuvres: An appetizer, as olives, celery, etc.

Host: A person who extends hospitality to others, usually in his own home.

Hotel Tray: Large oval tray.

Jardinière: A mixture of diced vegetables used in soups or as garnishing for meat dishes.

Julienne: Shredded or cut in fine strips.

Jus: Juice.

Lard: Bacon or pork fat.

Live One: A good table.

Lyonnaise: Cooked with onions.

Maître d': Dining room host.

Maître d'Hôtel: 1. A headwaiter or steward. 2. The manager or proprietor of a hotel. 3. Having a sauce of melted butter, parsley and lemon juice or vinegar.

Marinate: To steep meat, fish in a prepared liquid.

Marmite: The stockpot. A copper, iron or earthenware vessel used for making soup stock. Originally a French iron pot used for pot-au-feu.

Meringue: Egg white and sugar beaten together.

Monkey Dish: Small all-purpose dish.

Mousse: Light, airy dish, usually containing beaten egg whites or whipped cream for dessert (chocolate mousse), or meat, poultry or fish, finely ground and served in a mold for the main dish.

Nesselrode: A pudding containing chestnuts.

Open Station: A station that has not been assigned to a particular waiter.

Parfait: Frozen or chilled dessert, usually layered.

Pâté: An appetizer; common one is liver.

Pâté de Foie Gras: Well known delicacy prepared from the livers of fat geese,

Petits Fours: Fancy small filled cakes.

Poisson: Fish.

Poulet: Chicken.

Ragout: A stew with pieces of meat and a number of vegetables in a rich, thick gravy.

Ramekins: Tarts filled with cheese. Also individual earthenware baking dishes.

Réchaud: Chafing dish.

Roquefort: French cheese used in salad dressing.

Roux: A mixture of butter and flour used for thickening.

Sauerbraten: A beef dish made with marinated beef roast and sour cream.

Stroganoff: Beef tenderloin cut into strips, browned and then sour cream added.

Sauté: Fried lightly and quickly in a little hot fat while being frequently turned over.

Soufflé: A cream dish into which beaten egg whites are folded and then baked.

Stiff: A free table, no tip.

Stir Fry: Uniformly sliced meats or vegetables quickly stir fried in one of two tablespoons of hot oil, usually in a wok.

Table d'Hôte: A complete meal served at a restaurant or hotel, the price of the entire meal being determined by the price of the entrée one chooses. Compare À La Carte.

Tournedos: Small steaks which should be from the fillet.

Underliner: A dish used under another bowl or dish. A show plate.

Vinaigrette: Marinade or salad dressing of vinegar, oil, pepper, and herbs.

Wine Basket or Cradles: A basket so constructed that the wine bottles lie on their sides (red wines).

Wine List: Wines classified by country, vintage and price on a separate list from the menu.

Terminology Used in Food Preparation

1. Pan fry—Cook in small amount of fat.
   Sauté—To brown quickly in a small amount of fat, turning frequently.
   Stir fry—Uniformly sliced meats or vegetables, quickly stir in one or two tablespoons of hot oil, usually in a wok.

2. Dice—Cut in cubes.
   Mince—Cut or chop into very small pieces.

3. Simmer—To cook in liquid at a temperature of about 185 degrees F. Bubbles form slowly and break below the surface.

4. Blend—To mix thoroughly two or more ingredients.
   Cream—To mix one or more foods until smooth and creamy, usually applies to fat and sugar.

5. Chill—To place in the refrigerator until cooled to 40 to 45 degrees F.
   Cool—To lower the temperature.

6. Boil—To cook in liquid until bubbles rise continuously and break on the surface.
   Parboil—To boil until partially cooked.

7. Beat—To make a mixture smooth using an up-and-down motion.
   Whip—To beat rapidly cream, eggs, and gelatin dishes to incorporate air and increase volume.

8. Brush—To spread melted fat with a pastry brush.
   Dot—To cover with small particles, as to dot with butter.

9. Cut—To divide food into small pieces.
   Cut-in—To break fat into small particles by using two knives or a pastry blender.

10. Blanche—To dip into boiling water making skins easy to remove or to precook.
    Scald—To heat to a temperature just below the boiling point.
    Braise—To brown well in a little hot fat, then simmer in a little liquid, then cover until tender.

Review—Know Your Products (Chapter 35)
Fill in the blanks with correct answer from the list:
(Answers are contained in Appendix C, pages 225–229)

crêpe	gratuity	roux
bouillabaisse	carte du jour	entrée
wine list	host	maître d'
bon appétit	à la king	à la carte
bill of fare	table d'hôte	

1. A list of dishes provided at a meal is called the
   _____.

2. A thin pancake is also known as a
   _____.

3. The main dinner course is an _____.
4. Cooked in a cream sauce, with pimento or green pepper, mushrooms, etc. is _____.
5. A gift, usually of money, given in return for services rendered, is a _____.
6. A person who extends hospitality to others is a

_____.

7. On the menu, when each item has a separate price it is

_____.

8. A good appetite to you:

_____.

9. A dining room host is a

_____.

10. A mixture of butter and flour used for thickening is a

_____.

11. A fish soup with five or six varieties of fish and shellfish simmered together is _____.
12. Menu of the day is _____.
13. A complete meal served at a restaurant or hotel, the price of the entire meal being determined by the price of the entrée one chooses is called

_____.

14. Wines classified by country, vintage and price are on a separate list from the menu called a

_____.

Food Preparation
Fill in the blanks with correct answer from list:
(Answers are contained in Appendix C, pages 225–229)

sauté	whip	blanche
mince	scald	boil
braise	blend	
parboil	pantry	

1. To brown well in a little hot fat, then simmer in a little liquid, then cover until tender is to

    _____.

2. To cook in small amount of fat is to

    _____.

3. To cook in liquid until bubbles rise continuously and break on the surface is to _____.

4. To dip into boiling water making skins easy to remove or to precook is to _____.

5. To boil until partly cooked is to

    _____.

6. To brown quickly in a small amount of fat, turning frequently is to _____.

7. To heat to a temperature just below the boiling point is to _____.

8. To beat rapidly cream, eggs, and gelatin dishes to incorporate air and increase volume is to

    _____.

9. To mix thoroughly two or more ingredients is to

    _____.

10. To cut or chop into very small pieces is to

    _____.

36

"The Real World" Psychology in Service

When you serve the public, you are dealing with all types of people—some very nice and some not so nice. If you are serving a person who treats you badly, you must understand that he/she is the one with the personal problem. It is a psychological fact that a person who tries (and many times succeeds) to intimidate is basically insecure and covers up his insecurity by trying to act superior.

Don't Retaliate . . . all you do, then, is win the battle and lose the war. Treat him/her professionally. If you want to be in control of the situation, just imagine that person sitting in the chair in their underwear. Now, isn't that a funny scene? How can you not smile?

Your face is a mirror. Smile at people and they smile back. In most cases when the guest is unhappy and you try your darndest to please him/her, if you are sympathetic and try to solve the problem, he/she will usually be more understanding.

America is a wonderful country. We cheer for the underdog. Remember Rocky? When you handle the situation professionally, you will feel better about yourself and will truly be a professional.

How can you avoid most negative situations? Ninety percent of the problems of unhappy guests can be resolved by a professional attitude and the use of techniques advocated throughout this manual. One key technique used most assuredly to avoid a negative experience is to *check back to the table within the first minute after the food is served.* Again, this is a **Key Point** in service!

Ask, with genuine concern, "Are your dinners prepared the way you like?", and, "Is there anything else I can get for you right now?" Also, if a guest has ordered a steak, stand at the table and ask politely, "Would you please cut into your steak so you'll be sure it's done the way you like?" This is a key point in service, making extra sure that everything was prepared properly and everything that was ordered is there. What good is it to return to the table when the food is half or three quarters done. It's too late to solve the problem then, isn't it? Ninety-six percent of your guests won't complain and 90 percent don't come back.

The Formula for Success

Do you realize that you are the master of your own destiny? You can make your life or you can break it. If you want to be successful, it's really very simple. Find something you love to do and work at it. This is the real world. Where else can you have the opportunity to be in business for yourself, with no financial investment, no overhead, no risk? When you are a professional server, you are an independent contractor. The harder and smarter you work, the more benefits you get. Guaranteed! This means money in your pocket every day. The rewards come immediately after the service. This is great positive reinforcement.

Remember the boy scout motto, "Be prepared." In the food service business, being prepared means knowing your product (the menu), learning the techniques to do your job most efficiently and professionally (carrying trays, changing ash trays, knowing who gets the food without asking, etc. And most importantly, having a positive and genuinely friendly attitude. This is the formula for success.

Advancement Opportunities

Being a professional server has many advantages over other jobs because of the opportunities for advancement. Most restaurant operators promote from within the organization. If you set your sights on being a restaurant manager, the opportunities are there. It's up to you.

After reading this manual and answering all the questions at the end of each chapter, you are well on your way to understanding this business. But all the schooling and education don't mean a thing if you don't get the job. Are you ready for the interview? Remember, you've got only one chance to make a good first impression. If your prospective employer asks, "If 10 people apply for this job, why should I hire you?", what would be your answer?

GOOD LUCK!

Taking a Breather

We sincerely hope that by now you have learned something from our experience and observations. Many of the ideas in this manual can be incorporated into your restaurant set-up as you and your boss see fit. We purposely left many of our own ideas in this book for your use. Ed Solomon has won many national and state awards for merchandising and promotion and menu awards also on both levels. He is willing to exchange ideas or will answer any questions or help with any problems you might have. If you wish additional information, write to:

Professional Hospitality Consultants
c/o Ed Solomon
36214 Dellwood Road
Grafton, Ohio 44044
or Call: (216) 926-2608
or (216) 282-3133

And so for now—Good Bye and Good Luck, Honorable One.

Appendix A

Training Restaurant Personnel—The Key to Success!

How do you create an atmosphere of warmth, hospitality, and professionalism seen so often in successfully run operations? The answer is in caring enough for your employees to provide them with the tools they need to learn their trade.

For more information regarding the purchase of:
1. Service Training Manuals
2. Policy Manual Outlines
3. Orientation Checklists
4. A 7-Day Training Program

5. Hiring Questionnaires
6. Evaluation Forms
7. Food, Cocktail, Wine Breakdown Forms (to be filled in by you)

Contact:

Shelley Solomon Prueter
Professional Hospitality Consultants
36214 Dellwood Road
Grafton, Ohio 44044
Or phone (216) 926-2608

Listed below are a few testimonials from restaurant and hotel operators who have had the services and seminars offered by Ms. Prueter's company:

"This note is to inform you of my personal, unqualified endorsement of the training program for waiters and waitresses presented by your company."

"Due to the fine training by your company, we could not imagine opening another Springer hotel without you!"

Editor's Note:

This competency analysis profile is provided by James Brown, Assistant Director of Crawford County Area Vocational Technical School in Meadville, PA.

The utilization of Mr. Brown's suggestions solves major training problems for you. The *training package is now complete.*

The School Connection

We realize most schools are food preparation oriented and service to the guest has been a secondary concern.

However, if the students are to fulfill their career objectives of managing or owning their own restaurant they need to be aware of the importance of the "Heart of the House"/"front of the House" connection.

Did you know that poor or indifferent service to the guests is the number one complaint of those who eat in restaurants?

Included in the book are procedures that will eliminate 95 percent of the guests complaints and turn a "just a job" into a profitable career for the knowledgeable and enthusiastic waitperson.

I suggest contacting local restaurant operators who are involved with the school and use their menus in the role playing service programs the students get the feel of how the order should be taken and delivered *professionally*.

If you, the instructor, have any questions or suggestions on the implementation of this program contact:

Ed Solomon, Director of Training
36214 Dellwood Road
Grafton, Ohio, 44044
Fax (216) 236–8284

Introduction

The hospitality industry depends on quality service to the customer. Repeat business is the essence of success. Proper training in the twelve steps to service is difficult to achieve. However Ed Solomon has provided the tools to insure success. These twelve "moments of truth" are key points to the enhancement of the guests' dining experience.

Competency based instructional material objectives are clearly written and supported by Performance Assessment Forms.

Additional instructions are provided through our video tape "It Pays To Be A Pro." It demonstrates the appropriate procedures to succeed in the hospitality industry and a manual that explains the fine points of quality service. Step-by-step examples of what the server should say to serve effectively and sell are also included. "A picture is worth a thousand words, but a video is worth a million." . . . The National Restaurant Association.

These tools will help the teacher provide quality instruction to students interested in hospitality and restaurant service. The lesson plan and assessments forms are included, leaving little for teacher preparation. A certificate that can be reproduced by the teacher can be provided to the student who successfully performs the skills demonstrated in the lessons. Contact the author for a free sample of a certificate of completion.

Effective Service Scenario

The Restaurant Association did a survey of who was in charge of the dining experience. The server said the guest, because many times the guest was chasing the server for food items. The guests felt the server was in charge because the server, many times, was controlling the speed of the service. For example, the guest might want leisurely service and was served too quickly. How do we solve this problem? Who is in charge of the dining experience? The guest? The server? The answer is *both!*

Use the analogy of playing tennis. The server hits the ball (the decision) into the guests' court and then the guests make their decisions based on their needs and wants. This is KEY.

By communicating in this manner with the guests it takes the indecision out of the dining experience and gives the server the direction that s/he needs to give professional service.

Do say: "Good Evening, welcome to _____. Our features today are _____ and _____." Quote the prices and describe the features. "We have an excellent variety of appetizers, our most popular is the _____ or another popular appetizer is the _____ or our soup of the day is _____. The chef makes excellent soups. I've tasted them and they are delicious."

Don't say: "Would you like an appetizer?" Remember, you are a salesperson.

Guest: (may say) "We will have an order of _____ and a bowl of _____ soup."

Do say: After serving the appetizers say, "Would you like to *relax* (key word) with your appetizers or would you like me to take your dinner order?" The guests might give you the rest of the food order at this time. (Hit the ball [decision] into their court.

If they are ready to order, or when they have had time to relax and are ready to order, repeat the features of the day. Also quote the prices and let them know what is included. Be sure to mention if your restaurant has signature items that are unique.

Repeat the order as you write it down. Use abbreviations to save time. Leave out the vowels. For example, shrimp cocktail could be abbreviated SC or SH CK. Have you given them the options so they can make the decisions? You put the ball in their court. You are letting them know you are a caring professional.

The guest might say: "We would like to relax." If you observe they aren't ready to order, don't be pushy. Back off. When they close their menus, that is usually the sign that they are ready to order.

Do say: (The decision is in their court) With a smile say warmly, "would you like me to take your dinner order now?"

They will probably say: "Yes we are ready to order." Ask warmly, "Would you like me to repeat the features?"

Do say: "Our features today are 1. _____ 2. _____ and 3. _____." Quote prices too, and let them know what is included. Also, mention and describe the restaurants signature items.

Do repeat the order as you write it down. Use abbreviations to save time.

After you have led the guests through the food ordering procedure:

Do say: "Do you prefer your beverage now or with your dinner?" If coffee is ordered, ask "Would you like it now, or with your dinner?" Mark your order pad accordingly. All cold beverages are automatically served (Coke, iced tea, milk, etc.) with the dinner.

After serving the food, observe the table, do they need water? Additional beverage? Clean ash trays? More bread and butter? Ketchup? Steak sauce? Anything additional with the dinners?

Use the word happy, "I'd be happy to bring you some more bread and butter if you like." Remember, the willingness to serve is just as important as the service itself.

Watch your timing with both guests and the kitchen. It's crucial. Read your operation. Are the cooks fast? Slow?

If you feel there is a kitchen service problem, inform your manager or supervisor on duty before it becomes a major problem. Don't wait, because it leads to unhappy guests and negative word of mouth.

Now comes the Key Point in service. Get back to your guests within the *first minute.*

Do Say: "Is your dinner prepared to your satisfaction?"

Don't say: "How is everything?" This turns people off and they feel you don't really want to know.

"How is everything?" and "Was everything all right?" are meaningless questions, so meaningless that the guest is not expected to give an honest answer. The guest will normally swallow his criticism. If you truly want to know if the party is satisfied, you have the professional responsibility to get back *within the first minute* to solve the problem if there is a problem. Ninety-six percent of unhappy guests don't complain and 90 percent don't come back. How about negative word of mouth?

You can solve 95 percent of your problems if you get back within the *first minute* and *use the correct words.*

Check the table. Do they need ketchup, condiments, a beverage refill? This is part of being a professional. Be aware and anticipate their needs. If you have covered every base, then ask:

Do say: "Is there anything else you need?" The decision is in their court. They will probably say everything is fine, or, if they need something, this is the time to serve their needs.

Don't forget your guests! They might be in good shape and then decide they want some more sour cream for their baked potato or more cream for their coffee. The point is to be available. *When the hand goes up, the tip goes down. Be there first!*

Don't remove dinner plates until everyone is finished, unless requested to do so by the guest or unless they put their silverware on the plate. If they do that, politely ask them, "Would you like me to remove your plate?" (The decision is back in their court).

Do say: "We have a dessert tray that I'll bring over. I hope you left some room." Or suggest by saying, "We have some excellent desserts. Our most popular is _____," or "My favorite is _____." Be sure to describe them. (The ball is now in their court.) They will let you know which direction they want to take. Don't take rejection personally. Accept their decision graciously.

If the guests are too full:

Do say: "How about one piece with two forks?" (For two people)

Bring an extra fork automatically because the person who didn't order will usually take one or two bites.

Do say: "Would you like me to refill your coffee?" (Caring) Check cream and sugar. If you feel they are now ready for their check, address the host (eye contact, smile) and say, "Would you like me to bring the check?"

Be sure to total the check away from the table. Don't keep them waiting for the check. This is just before they leave their tip and it could be the last impression they get of your restaurant.

When you put the check down with the tip tray, make eye contact and say (sincerely), "Thank you. It has been a pleasure serving you."

Server: Observe the other guests. Are they ready for a

refill on coffee? Ask (politely, make eye contact): "Would you care for some hot coffee?" By doing this you are letting them know you care.

If cash is placed on the tip tray, mention the amount (in a low tone) out of $20, out of $40, or whatever the amount.

This type of error rarely happens, but could be a problem, solve it before it becomes a problem.

On a charge, fill out the information and bring it back to the table.

Do say: "Thank you, Mr. Jones. (Use the name you see on the credit card), would you please sign by the X." Give him/her a copy.

If they are relaxing, don't be pushy.

Make eye contact (sweep the guests) if you still have their attention and say, "I hope we'll see you again and please ask for me to serve you."

Technical point in service—When you clear their dinner plates (from left side with the left hand so you don't have your elbow and arm pit under their noses) also clear all other dishes.

The only thing left on the table, at this time, is the water glass, coffee cup or beverage glass and a clean ash tray.

If you have smokers, replace the ash tray when it contains two or three butts (company standard). Provide a clean ashtray while they are eating dinner. Wipe it out so it is clear of ashes.

Please Note:

This script is for non-alcoholic dinner service.

If you have questions, please contact:
    Ed Solomon, Director
    Professional Hospitality Center
    36214 Dellwood Road.
    Grafton, OH 44044
    (216) 926–2608 or
    (216) 282–3133
    Fax (216) 236–8284

Script for Service with Alcoholic Beverages

This is an optional service scenario which teaches the sales techniques for selling alcoholic beverages.

The Restaurant Association did a survey of who was in charge of the dining experience. The servers said the guest, because many times the guest was chasing the server for food items and was controlling the speed of the service. The guest said the server because he/she may want speedy service and it was slow or they might want leisurely service and it was too fast. How do we solve this problem? Who is in charge of the dining experience? The guest? The server? The answer is *both!*

Use the analogy of playing tennis. The server hits the ball (the decision) into the guests' court and they make the decisions based on their needs and wants. This is the key.

Do say: "Good evening. Welcome to _____. Our features today are _____, _____ and _____." Quote prices and describe specials. "We have some great specialty house beverages before dinner. We feature _____ and _____, or do you have your own personal choice?" Pause for a reply. Get the cocktail order and now offer appetizers.

Key Point: Repeat the cocktail order as you write (abbreviate it down. Example: Strawberry Margarita—ST MRG. This eliminates serving the wrong beverage which makes you and the organization look bad. Also repeat (and abbreviate) the appetizer order.

Do say: "We have an excellent variety of appetizers. Our most popular are the _____ and _____ and _____." (Pause for reply.) Also repeat (and abbreviate) the appetizer order. The guest will let you know what appetizer they want or if they want no appetizers.

Guest: "We will have an order of _____ and an order of _____."

Drop off the appetizer order in the kitchen and pick up cocktails. Be sure to serve cocktails to the proper persons.

Don't say: "Would you like an appetizer?" Remember, you are a salesperson!

Do say: after serving the appetizers—"Would you like to *relax* with your appetizers or would you like me to take your dinner order?" (*Relax* is the key emphasis.)

If the guests say, "We would like to relax," observe the cocktail situation. **Key point:** Eyeball the table for the person with the least amount of alcohol in his/her glass. Make eye contact and say (very pleasantly) "Would you like a fresh _____ (specific beverage). In other words, if he/she had ordered a JB & Soda, make eye contact and say "Would you like a *fresh* (buzzword) JB & Soda?" Then sweep the rest of the party, smile, nod your head (positively up and down) and say, "Would you like *fresh* (there's that word again) beverages?" If they are not ready, they will let you know. Remember the tennis analogy? You are hitting the ball (the decision) into their court.

Don't say: "Would you like another drink?" Negative point in service because a sensitive guest may believe you are implying that s/he is an alcoholic. "You want *another* drink?" Can you see the difference?

By this time they will probably be ready to order dinner.

Do say: (The decision is in their court.) "Would you like me to take your dinner order now?"

Do repeat the order as you write it down. Use abbreviations as they save time.

After you have taken their dinner order:

Do say: "A glass of _____ (specific wine) would go well with your dinner or bottle of _____ would go well with your dinners. (Tennis ball is back in their court, they will let you know their decision).

This is not too pushy but rather is making them aware of features that would add a positive touch to their dining experience.

After serving the dinners, observe the table. Do they need water? Additional beverage? Clean ash tray? More bread and butter? Do they need ketchup? Steak sauce?

Use the word happy, "I'd be happy to bring you some more bread and butter." Remember, the willingness to serve is just as important as the service itself. You tried, you gave them the option. You put the ball in their court. You are showing them you are a caring professional.

Watch the timing with both guests and the kitchen. It's crucial. Are the cooks fast? Slow? If you feel that there is a kitchen service problem, inform your manager or supervisor as soon as possible.

Key Point in Service: get back to the table after the guest has had two or three bites or within one minute and:

Do say: "Is your dinner prepared to your satisfaction" or " . . . the way you like it?" You solve 95 percent of your problems if you get back within the first minute and use the correct words.

Don't say: "How is everything?" This turns people off and they feel, psychologically, that you don't really want to know. Do you realize that this is a meaningless query? It is so meaningless that your guests are not expected to give an honest answer.

Check the table. Do they need ketchup, condiments, a beverage refill? This is part of being a professional. Be aware. Anticipate their needs. If you feel you have covered every base, then ask:

Do say: "Is there anything else you need?" (The ball is back in their court.) They will probably say everything is fine.

Don't forget them! They might be in good shape and then decide that they want some more sour cream for their baked potato or more cream for their coffee. The point is to be available. When the hand goes up, the tip goes down. Be there first!

Don't remove dinner plates until everyone is finished, unless requested to do so by the guest or unless they put their silverware on the plate. If they do that, ask them politely "Would you like me to remove your plates?" (The tennis ball is back in their court.)

Do say: "We have a dessert tray that I'll bring over. I hope you left some room." Or suggest by saying, "We have some excellent desserts. Our most popular is _____." Or " . . . my favorite is _____." Describe the desserts.

Do say: "We also feature Kahlua and Cream to settle your dinner or maybe a Baileys on the rocks." (wait for a reply) (decisions in their court). I'll be happy to refill your coffee (caring) (check cream and sugar). If you feel they are now ready for their check, address the host (eye contact, smile) and say, "Would you like me to bring the check?" The above procedure will build sales, tips and result in guest satisfaction and repeat business.

Be sure to total the check away from the table. Don't keep them waiting for the check. This is just before they leave their tip and their last impression of the restaurant. Don't forget to smile.

When you put the check down with the tip tray, make eye contact and say (sincerely), "Thank you. It has been a pleasure serving you."

Server: Observe the other guests. Are they ready for a refill on coffee? Ask (politely, make eye contact): "Would you care for some hot coffee?" (By doing this you are letting them know you care, right?) if cash is placed on the tip tray, mention the amount (in a low tone) out of $20, out of $40, out of $50. This procedure eliminates any chance of error.

Many operations today let the server be her/his own bank. Don't make change at the table. If a cashier is used, announce the amount given to the cashier to eliminate the chance of error.

When you take money to the cashier, announce the amount back to her (or him) out of $20, out of $40, out of whatever the amount. This type of error rarely happens but could be problem. Solve it before it becomes a problem.

On a charge, fill out the information and bring it back to the table.

Do say: "Thank you, Mr. Jones. (Use the name you see on the credit card), would you please sign by the X." Give him/her a copy.

If they are relaxing, don't be pushy. Remember, they are your responsibility until they leave the restaurant.

Make eye contact (sweep the guests) if you still have their attention and say, "I hope we'll see you again and please ask for me to serve you."

Technical point in service—When you clear their dinner plates (from left side with the left hand so you don't have your elbow and arm pit under their noses) also clear all other dishes.

The only thing left on the table, at this time, is the water glass, coffee cup or beverage glass and a clean ash tray. If you have smokers, replace the ash tray when it contains two or three butts (company standard). Provide a clean ashtray while they are eating dinner. Wipe it out so it is clear of ashes.

If you have questions, please contact:

Professional Hospitality Center
Ed Solomon, Director of Training
36214 Dellwood Rd
Grafton, OH, 44044
(216) 926–2608 or
(216) 282–3133
Fax (216) 236–8284

Server
Job Description

Competency Guide

Competency: Provide quality service to restaurant guests.

Introduction:

Service is one of the oldest acts of hospitality in existence. It represents something special to your guest. To the guest, dining is the time of relaxation and companionship. Special precaution must be taken to insure that enjoyment of good food is not spoiled by careless service.

Good food is important, but good service is more important. It is the extra touch that satisfies the American hunger for prestige that goes with eating out, having a snack or just a cup of coffee. Good service can also improve the earnings of those who learn to provide it effectively and efficiently. The development of this competency will improve your success as an employee and put additional money in your pocket as a service provider.

Terminal Objective: Provide quality service to restaurant guest.

While working in an actual restaurant situation, you will provide quality customer service to the guests. Your performance will be evaluated by receiving "satisfactory" on all of the criteria on the performance assessment form provided.

Enabling Objectives:

- Prepare yourself and dining area for service.
- Greet the guest and take the order.
- Serve the guests.
- Clear soiled dishes.
- Practice sales techniques.
- Present the check and accept payment.

Resources and references.

Solomon, Ed, and Prueter, Shelley, *Service is an Honorable Profession, A complete study in American Service.* Grafton, Ohio, Professional Hospitality Center, 1973, revised 1979, 1987, 1990, 1996.

"It Pays to be a Pro!", a service training video by Ed Soloman.

Performance Assessment Form

Criteria:

In preparing to serve your guests:

1. Check for the features of the day
2. How are they prepared? Ingredients? Portion size?
3. Know the menu, prices, features of the day, and descriptions of the food listed.
4. Inspect the service areas and your station for cleanliness and table settings.
5. Check side work areas for adequate supplies and housekeeping.
6. Maintain appropriate personal appearance.

In taking the order from your guests:

7. Approach the table from the pivot point with a smile, good posture, a pleasant welcome and an introduction.
8. Present the menu, explain the features and suggest a beverage and/or appetizers.
9. Serve a glass of ice water before taking the order.
10. Speak clearly, softly and distinctly and make eye contact.
11. Take each order moving around the table in clockwise sequence.
12. Repeat the order to the guest as you write it down on the check.
13. Write legibly and abbreviate as appropriate.
14. Identify the location of each guest for proper service.

15. Use suggestive selling techniques.

In serving the guest:

16. Serve beverages from the right (except in booth service) with the right hand.
    A. Pour to the table.
    B. Use coffee underliner to shield guests.
    C. Serve cold beverages with dinner.
    D. Remove empty glasses from the right with the right hand.
17. Deliver bread and butter and/or appetizers.
18. Repeat the order as the items are served.
19. Serve from the left with the left hand.
20. Serve the main entrée directly in front of the guest, potato on the left, and vegetable on the right.
21. Return to the table within one minute of service to ask if everything is prepared to the guest's satisfaction.
22. Ask if there is anything else needed at this time.

In clearing the table:

23. Clear plates and dishes as guests finish them from the left with your left hand.
24. Properly load the tray with weight concentrated on the middle or the side that will rest on the shoulder.
25. Remove the bread and butter plates last.
26. If all food is not eaten, offer a people bag or carry out box.
27. Refill coffee and sell desserts.

In presenting the checks:

28. Insure the check is clean and neat.
29. Check for readability and errors.
30. Present the check in a timely manner.
31. Present the check face down in front of the host or in the center of the table if you don't know who the host is.
32. Explain the payment procedures.
33. Offer to take care of the check.
34. Thank the guests and invite them to return.

Host-Hostess/ Supervisor
Job Description

Competency Guide

Competency: Perform the duties of the dining room host-hostess/supervisor

Introduction:

The dining room host-hostess/supervisor is responsible for the first impression the guest receives from the restaurant and the final satisfaction with the dining experience. The supervisor is the key to a successful operation in the dining room. His/her attitude toward the guest is reflected in all service personnel under his/her supervision. A supervisor's prime concern is guest satisfaction.

The first 30 seconds are very important in guest satisfaction. The guest's first impression of your restaurant can affect his/her appetite. Tact and good judgment are important traits for someone in this position.

Terminal Objective:

While working in an actual restaurant situation, you will provide supervision of the entire dining room operation to insure guest satisfaction. Your performance will be evaluated by receiving "satisfactory" on all of the criteria on the performance assessment form provided.

Resources and references:

Solomon, Ed, and Prueter, Shelley, *Service is an Honorable Profession, A complete study in American Service*. Grafton, Ohio, Professional Hospitality Center, 1973, revised 1979, 1987, 1990.

"It Pays to be a Pro!", a service training video by Ed Soloman. 36214 Dellwood Rd., Grafton, OH 44044.

Performance Assessment Form

Competency: Perform host-hostess/supervisor duties:

Criteria:

1. Inspect the appearance of food service employees.
2. Assign dining room stations and side work duties.
3. Check reservations for table set-ups.
4. Check supplies.
5. Check service stands for required items.
6. Check menus for appearance, specials of the day and correct information.
7. Check the dining room for cleanliness and appearance.
8. Plan ahead for guest seating to insure each serving.
9. Receive guests.
   a. Greet guests with a smile.
   b. Escort the guest to the table.
   c. Place the open menu before each guest and tell him the name of his server.
   d. Check table for appropriate set up.
10. Alert servers to their guests and any special needs.
11. Insure proper and efficient service.
    a. Keep the servers aware of guest needs.
    b. Take corrective action in private when necessary.
    c. Observe the food served for proper portion and quality.
    d. Apply suggestive selling.
    e. Have bussers clear and reset table promptly.
    f. Handle complaints and deal with difficult guests.

12. Take reservations.
13. Insure all dining room personnel have their breaks.
14. Insure that bussers and servers have performed their duties at closing.
15. Don't expect—inspect.

Busser
Job Description

Competency Guide

Competency: demonstrate proper procedure for bussing tables

Introduction:

The name bus boy comes from the Latin word omnibus, meaning many things at the same time. A busser's primary responsibility is the cleaning and resetting of tables after the guests have gone. Other jobs may include assisting guests and servers and maintaining cleanliness and order in the dining from and kitchen. Appearance and manners are of utmost importance. Speed and efficiency are also important. A fast, efficient busperson can increase the turnover in the restaurant, thus enabling the restaurant to serve more guests and increase revenues accordingly.

Terminal objective:

While working in a restaurant situation, you will clear and reset tables, assist the servers and guests, and insure proper cleanliness of the dining and kitchen areas. Your performance will be evaluated by receiving "satisfactory" on all of the criteria on the performance evaluation provided.

Resources and references:

Solomon, Ed, and Prueter, Shelley, *Service is an Honorable Profession, A complete study in American Service*. Grafton, Ohio, 1973, revised 1979, 1987, 1990.

"It Pays to be a Pro!", a service training video by Ed Soloman. 36214 Dellwood Rd., Grafton, OH 44044.

Performance Assessment Form

Competency: Demonstrate proper procedure for bussing tables.

Criteria:

When bussing tables:
1. Maintain a neat and clean personal appearance.
2. Be polite, well mannered and cheerful.
3. Clean and reset the tables after the guests have gone.
   a. Push all chairs in.
   b. Remove silverware first, placing it on the outer edge of the tray in one direction.
   c. Remove glasses four at a time holding them at the base.
   d. Stack all like items together and remove them.
   e. Collect napkins and place them on the tray.
   f. Balance the tray for ease when carrying.
   g. Move the soiled dishes to the kitchen.
   h. Clean ashtray and remove refuse from the table.
   i. Brush crumbs to edge of table and pick up with cloth or brush.
   j. Check chairs for cleanliness and wipe.
   k. Reset the table for the next party.
4. Assist guests and waiters.
   a. Fulfill guests needs when the waitress is busy.
   b. Fill water glasses and refill coffee cups.

    c. Empty ash trays.

    d. Keep cups, saucers, glasses, ice and silverware stocked.

    e. Make coffee.

    f. Stock paper supplies and food supplies.

    g. Return empty trays and racks to proper storage.

5. Save time and steps when performing duties.

6. Maintain cleanliness and order in the dining room and kitchen.

7. Assist in closing.

    a. Wipe down all tables.

    b. Assist servers with side work.

    c. Remove and store tray stands.

    d. Check with supervisor for instructions.

Appendix B

Comprehensive Server Test

(Answers are contained in Appendix C, pages 230–231)

True or False

1. T F   Service is an Honorable Profession.
2. T F   The guest is not always right but s/he is never wrong.
3. T F   The first four minutes of contact with the personnel of a restaurant is the period where guests form lasting opinions of the operation.
4. T F   Most guests tip the same amount all the time.
5. T F   Excellent service pays off only if it is quality service.
6. T F   If you are doing sidework and the guest signals, finish what you are doing first.
7. T F   For booths, we use a type of service known as the French method.

8. T F It doesn't matter if you reach in front of the guest and have your elbow near their face.

9. T F All beverage are served from the right side with either hand.

10. T F It doesn't hurt to stick your fingers in the glass when clearing tables.

11. T F Keep your back as straight as possible as you straighten your legs when you lift a tray.

12. T F If two tables are seated at the same time, don't ignore either.

13. T F The key to selling is to do the thinking for the guest and think positive.

14. T F You don't have to repeat the order as you write it down.

15. T F Learn how long it takes to prepare food items.

16. T F Sixty percent of your customers don't know what they are going to eat until they look at the menu.

17. T F If guests ask what's good, tell them everything.

18. T F Steps are time and time is money.

19. T F Timing is the most difficult step in food service.

20. T F When opening the Champagne, twist the cork and not the bottle.

21. T F The rule of thumb—White wines go with seafood and chicken, red wines with meat and rose wine with either.

22. T F If you're not proud of it, don't serve it.

23. T F If steak is ordered, don't worry about how it's cooked.

24. T F All beverages are served with dinner.

25. T F When presenting the check after lunch or dinner, it's important to make contact, smile and say, "It's been a pleasure serving you and please come back again soon."

Fill in the Blanks

Words for *Fill In The Blanks*

Serve	Balance	Proud
Private	Public	Blend
You	Quickly	Don't
Hot	Dessert	Pan-fry
Tip	Party Book	Tip
Twelve	Entrée	Supervisor
Waiting	One	Host/Hostess

At lunch, the check is presented when the guest has finished his (1)_____ and his (2)_____ has been refilled.

Don't keep the guest (3)_____ for his check.

Bring food (4)_____ for the children.

The most effective way for the guest to be informed is through (5)_____.

The willingness to (6)_____ is just as important as the (7)_____ itself.

The server works her tables as (8)_____ by coordinating the order.

It takes at least (9)_____ trips for an average dinner.

When working a party, check with the (10)_____ or your (11)_____ for details.

The name busboy comes from the Latin word (12)_____.

Key point in carrying a tray is (13)_____ the tray so it doesn't (14)_____.

The (15)_____ is the key to a successful dining experience.

A supervisor should criticize the employee in
(16)_____.
If one person comes to eat in your restaurant, don't say
"Only (17)_____."
Praise the server in (18)_____.
The main dinner in the (19)_____.
A gift given in return for service rendered is called a
(20)_____.
To cook in small amounts of fat is to
(21)_____.
To mix thoroughly two ingredients is to
(22)_____.
If you're not (23)_____ of it,
(24)_____ serve it.
Serve cold foods cold and hot foods
(25)_____.

Multiple Choice

Circle the Correct Answer

1. A thin pancake is called a

   a. Entrée
   b. Crêpe
   c. Du jour
   d. Turnover

2. A dining room host is called a

   a. Maître d'
   b. King
   c. Table d'hôte
   d. Boss

3. A mixture of butter and flour is called a(n)

   a. À la king
   b. Roux
   c. À la carte
   d. Bouillabaisse

4. The hostess prime concern is
   a. Suggestion selling
   b. Guest satisfaction
   c. Turnover
   d. Carrying trays
5. The bus person should
   a. Pour coffee if needed
   b. Be able to cook
   c. Tend bar
   d. None of the above
6. When serving a party allow _____ inches per person.
   a. 20
   b. 10
   c. 36
   d. 24
7. Serve dessert to _____ first.
   a. Men
   b. Women
   c. The head table
   d. Closest to the kitchen
8. When co-workers work together, it's called the _____ system.
   a. Supervisor
   b. Special
   c. Service
   d. Buddy
9. Sell dessert by
   a. Presenting the tray
   b. Describing them
   c. Telling guest your favorite
   d. All of the above

10. Total your check
    a. On the table
    b. At the table
    c. Away from the table
    d. None of the above

11. When you put the check down
    a. Smile
    b. Make eye contact
    c. Say thank you
    d. All of the above

12. When the guest pays by credit card
    a. S/he will place card on tip tray
    b. Don't say anything
    c. Automatically add the tip
    d. Ask if you can add the tip

13. When serving dessert, the fork should
    a. Be on the left
    b. Be on the right
    c. Be in the center
    d. Not be on the table

14. When refilling water
    a. Don't bother
    b. Pick up the glass
    c. Pour to the table
    d. Give a fresh glass

15. When serving coffee
    a. Check for cream
    b. Check for sugar
    c. Is it hot?
    d. All of the above

16. When steak is ordered
    a. Check back after one minute
    b. Check back after four minutes
    c. Don't worry if it's done right
    d. Ask them to cut it in the middle as soon as you serve it
17. When selling appetizers
    a. Suggest specific appetizers
    b. Ask if they want appetizers
    c. Don't ask
    d. Let them ask you
18. When you tell them the specials
    a. Don't mention price
    b. Don't describe specials
    c. Make a face if you don't like it
    d. Quote prices
19. When you take the dinner order
    a. Repeat it as you write it down
    b. Abbreviate
    c. Make eye contact
    d. All of the above
20. How soon should you check back to see if the food is prepared to the guests satisfaction?
    a. Never
    b. Within 1 minute
    c. When they are done
    d. Within 4 minutes
21. When you pick up your order in the kitchen
    a. Just pick it up and go
    b. Don't worry about food appearance
    c. Don't complain if something is wrong
    d. Make sure it's complete

22. Timing is key when putting in your order so
    a. Bring it out even if they aren't ready
    b. Don't worry if it's too long
    c. Make sure your guests are ready to be served
    d. If there's a problem, don't tell the manager because s/he might get upset

23. Key points in timing
    a. A well done steak will slow down the service
    b. The number of people in the dining room is a factor
    c. The ability of the cook is a factor
    d. All of the above

24. Your face is a mirror—smile at people and they smile back
    a. Is a silly quote
    b. Makes the food taste better
    c. Isn't important at all
    d. People don't care

25. Service is an Honorable Profession
    a. Means you should take pride in your service
    b. Means you should take pride in yourself
    c. Your guests want professional, caring service
    d. All of the above

Circle the Correct Answer
More than one answer could be correct

1. We have an excellent variety of appetizers. Our most popular is _____ or my favorite is _____.
   Don't Say   Do Say

2. Would you like an appetizer?
   Don't Say   Do Say

3. After serving the appetizer, use the buzz word
   "_____."
   Enjoy   Relax

4. Who is in charge of the dining experience?
   The Guest   The Server

5. When taking the food order, use the analogy of
   _____.
   Playing Tennis   Playing Basketball

6. _____ the order as you write it down.
   Don't Repeat   Repeat

7. The _____ to serve is just as important as the food itself.
   Willingness   Caring

8. Don't say "
   Is your dinner prepared the way you like?"
   How is everything?"

9. Do say "Is
   everything OK?"
   there anything else you need?"

10. When the hand goes up
    the tip goes down.
    they are probably just waving at a friend.

11. Don't remove dinner plates
    until everyone is finished.
    unless requested to do so by the guest.

12. Knowledge builds your
    tips.   self esteem.

13. Think of yourself in the restaurant industry as a
    slave.   salesperson.

14. Don't say
    have a nice day.   come back soon.

15. When you put the check down,
    say it's been a pleasure serving you.
    explain payment procedures.

16. After the check is paid
    ignore them.
    keep your eye on them in case they need additional service.

17. Your objective in a restaurant is
    to make money.   please the guests.

18. Knowledge of the _____ will aid your guests.
    Menu   preparation of food
    specials   all three topics

19. Serve beverages (except for booth service),
    from the right.   from the left.

20. When serving beverages
    pick up the cup or glass.
    pour to the table.

21. A bus person's objective is
    to assist the servers and guests.
    to just set and clear tables and ignore everything else.

22. It is important that the bus person
    maintain a neat and clean personal appearance.
    save time and steps when performing duties.

23. The prime objective of the hostess/supervisor is
    to crack the whip on the servers.
    provide supervision and leadership.
    to insure guest satisfaction.

24. When the customer gives you a bad time
    ignore them.
    argue back.
    don't retaliate.

25. Your face is a mirror
    smile at people and they smile back.
    if you're grouchy, the customer could be grouchy also.

Appendix C

Review and Test Answers

CHAPTERS 1, 2, and 3

1. SERVICE
2. PEOPLE
3. FOOD, SERVICE
4. 30 SECONDS, LASTING OPINIONS
5. COMPLIMENTS
6. WAGES
7. TRAINING
8. SERVICE, ATTENTION, PRESTIGE, ADVENTURE
9. YOU
10. OPINION
11. LOOK, ACT, TALK, THEIR NEEDS
12. CHARM, PERSONALITY, APPEARANCE
13. PERSONAL PROBLEMS
14. MOOD
15. EQUALLY
16. QUIETLY, TACTFULLY
17. KIDDING AROUND
18. CLIQUES
19. SMOTHER
20. LOOK
21. SMILE
22. SPEAK, MUMBLE
23. TONE
24. SIRS, MA'AMS
25. QUIETLY, PROMPTLY
26. WRONG
27. PERSONALITY
28. NAME
29. GREETINGS, SERVICE
30. SMILE, PLEASANT ATTI-TUDE
31. GUEST

CHAPTERS 4, 5, 6, and 7

1. TO INSURE PROMPTNESS
2. PERCENTAGE
3. TIP
4. EXTRA
5. PROFESSIONAL
6. QUALITY
7. SLOPPY
8. INSIDE
9. HAIR SPRAY
10. ATTRACTIVE, SMILE
11. EAR
12. GUM
13. EYES
14. SIGNALS
15. NEEDS, FIRST
16. BEING IGNORED
17. IGNORE
18. MANNER
19. SHOUTING
20. NOTICE, SERVICE
21. WAITRESS, HOSTESS

CHAPTERS 8, 9, 10, and 11

1. SUPERVISOR
2. MENU, PRICES, SPECIALS, DAY, FOODS
3. CRUMBS
4. LIGHT
5. COVER
6. CLOTH
7. INCH
8. TWELVE
9. WATER GLASS
10. BREAD AND BUTTER PLATE
11. COCKTAIL
12. BOWL OF TEASPOON
13. HANDLES, BLADES, TINES, BOWLS
14. NAPKIN
15. LEFT

16. FIVE
17. FOOD CART
18. HOST OR HOSTESS
19. CLOCKWISE
20. FAMILY
21. EXACT OPPOSITE
22. RIGHT, LEFT
23. OFF HAND
24. INSIDE, LEFT
25. OUTSIDE, RIGHT
26. TOUCHING, MOVE OUT
27. RIGHT

CHAPTER 12

1. ELBOW
2. RIGHT, RIGHT
3. LEFT
4. LEFT
5. ORALLY, WRITE
6. ONE, OTHER, THE TABLE
7. RIGHT, RIGHT
8. ENTREE, FRONT
9. COLD, HOT

CHAPTER 13

1. HANDLING, SPILLAGE, BREAKAGE
2. HEAVY DISHES IN CENTER OF TRAY, EDGE OF TRAY THAT WILL BE PLACED ON SHOULDER
3. SAUCERS
4. UNDERLINERS
5. TURNED IN
6. 1/2"
7. BOTH
8. 8
9. DINING ROOM
10. KNEES, SHOULDER
11. BACK, LEGS

CHAPTERS 14 AND 15

1. WATER, SMILE, SIX

2. WATER
3. CENTER
4. GOOD EVENING, BE WITH YOU SHORTLY
5. THINKING, CUSTOMER, POSITIVELY
6. VERBALLY, WRITE
7. WINE, LIQUOR, MIXED DRINKS, CREME DRINKS, BEER
8. 4, COCKTAIL NAPKIN
9. RIGHT
10. HALF
11. WOULD YOU LIKE YOUR COCKTAILS REFRESHED?
12. KINDNESS
13. COCKTAIL, DINNER ORDER
14. WOULD YOU LIKE TO RELAX A WHILE
15. COFFEE CUP, WATER GLASS
16. RIGHT, LEFT
17. FOOD SERVICE
18. IDENTIFICATION

CHAPTER 16

1. SALAD
2. LEMON WEDGE
3. LEMON WEDGE
4. FOUR
5. RIGHT
6. APPETIZERS, COCKTAIL GLASSES. SALAD BOWLS
7. WATER GLASSES
8. NEEDS
9. PREPARE

CHAPTER 17

1. EIGHTY PERCENT, MENU
2. HELP, EXTRAS
3. GUIDE
4. HURRY

5. ENTRÉE
6. DISTASTE
7. STEAK
8. WITH BLEU CHEESE
9. WITH DINNER OR LATER
10. COLD DRINKS
11. A BOTTLE OF WINE
12. LAST
13. VERBALLY
14. AT THE MENU
15. SMILE, THANK EACH OF
16. SALE
17. SUGGESTION SELLING
18. PRESOLD, CONFUSED, UNDECIDED
19. CARRY HIM THROUGH THE REST OF THE ORDER VERBALLY
20. TWO
21. POSITIVE
22. SELLING

CHAPTER 18

1. POSITION SYSTEM
2. MEMORIZE, ABBREVIA-TIONS
3. FOUR
4. STEPS, MONEY
5. POSITION SYSTEM I
6. POSITION SYSTEM II, GRID
7. LEFT
8. CHECK TRAY
9. DATE, TABLE NUMBER, SERVER NUMBER & NUM-BER OF PEOPLE
10. WHO, WHAT
11. GUESTS
12. EYE CONTACT, PLEASANT-LY, READY
13. RELAX, ENJOY
14. CLOCKWISE, PIVOT POINT, LEFT

15. VERTICALLY, HORIZON-
    TALLY
16. LINE, SPACE
17. DASH
18. COCKTAIL, APPETIZER,
    ENTRÉE, VEGETABLE,
    POTATO, EXTRA, SALAD,
    BEVERAGE, DESSERT

19.

1. w/w	achok	v parm	sp	gb	– –	lt.	c/w	– –
2. Xman Tw	– –	stp/m	bp/sb	gb	– –	fr	c/l	ches
3. mols	mozz	fl/r	mp/g	gb	s. mush	fr	mlk	– –
4. chab	pz sk	v pct	bp/p	– –	– –	o&v	c/w	rs ck

20. ONE CHECK
21. GRID, SEPARATE CHECKS
22. AMOUNT TENDERED,
    LEFT, CASH
23. MASTER, SEPARATE,
    TOTALS
24. THANK YOU

CHAPTER 19
1. TIMING
2. MENU
3. STEAK WELL DONE
4. BEFORE
5. MANAGER
6. CHECK
7. SOUR CREAM, BUTTER,
   COLE SLAW, APPETIZERS
8. RELISH TRAY, SALADS
9. RELISH TRAY
10. SURF & TURF, LOBSTER
11. HOT BREAD

CHAPTER 20
1. TABLE, RIGHT, LABEL
2. FIRMLY, CORK
3. BOTTLE
4. CORKSCREW, HOLDING
5. FLAT, BASKET, WINE
   GLASS
6. CHARGED, ELBOW

7. 2, 4
8. 1/4
9. CLOCKWISE, LEFT
10. 2/3, BREATHE
11. LIFT, TURN
12. WATER GLASS, COFFEE
    CUP
13. WHITE OR ROSE'

14. FISH OR CHICKEN, RED
    MEAT, EITHER
15. 2, TYPE
16. WE'RE OUT OF THIS,
    SUGGEST
17. YOU

CHAPTERS 21 AND 22
1. YOUR ORDER
2. HOT
3. CORRECT, COMPLETE,
   PREPARED
4. SERVING
5. GARNISHED
6. SPILLED
7. PROUD, SERVE
8. FIRST, COLD
9. HOT, WARM
10. IN FRONT OF A GUEST
11. BACK
12. STEAK
13. ON
14. CATSUP, FRENCH FRIES
15. ASH TRAYS
16. BREAD, BUTTER
17. HOW'S YOUR STEAK?
    DONE THE WAY YOU LIKE?
18. PREPARED
19. NOW

20. MAY I GET A PEOPLE'S BAG
21. MAIN PLATE, SIDE DISH
22. BREAD & BUTTER PLATES
23. WATER GLASSES, COFFEE CUPS, TEASPOONS

CHAPTERS 23 AND 24

1. COLD
2. RIGHT, RIGHT
3. BASE, DRINKING EDGE
4. 20 AFTER 12
5. UNDERLINER
6. SAUCER
7. SAUCER, WIPE DRY
8. POUR, TABLE
9. LEMON WEDGE
10. WORD PICTURE
11. POSITIVE, TWO
12. FRESH, FRESH
13. CENTER, LEFT
14. RIGHT
15. AFTER DINNER DRINK
16. GRASSHOPPER, KAHLUA & CREAM
17. COFFEE

CHAPTER 25

1. MAIN COURSE, COFFEE
2. DESSERT, COFFEE
3. FINISHED ORDERING
4. 3/4, REFILL
5. TOP, BOTTOM
6. NAME, TABLE NUMBER
7. PRICES
8. ON THE TABLE
9. AWAY
10. GRANTED, ALERT
11. MAY I TAKE THIS FOR YOU
12. REPEAT
13. COINS, TOP
14. TIP TRAY, SMILE, THANK YOU
15. SPOTLESS

16. LEGIBLE, CORRECT
17. WAITING
18. MASTER CHARGE, AMERICAN EXPRESS, DINERS, VISA
19. CHARGE

CHAPTERS 26 and 27

1. SPECIAL ATTENTION
2. FOOD
3. KIDDIE COCKTAILS
4. THE PARENT, CRACKERS
5. SMALL GLASSES
6. PATRONIZE, SATISFIED
7. GOOD WILL, FAVORABLE
8. SUPERVISOR
9. SERVICE
10. BIRTHDAYS, ANNIVERSARIES
11. YOU
12. CIGARETTES
13. SERVE, SERVICE
14. STEPS, EASIER WORK
15. BUDDY
16. ONE
17. TWELVE
18. EMPTY HANDED, KITCHEN
19. COLORED STIRRER
20. LEFT

CHAPTER 29

1. SUPERVISOR
2. 24
3. TIMING
4. APPETIZER, SALADS
5. APPETIZERS, SALADS, COCKTAIL GLASSES
6. RULES
7. COFFEE, WATER
8. ASH TRAYS
9. MAIN COURSE PLATES, MAIN COURSE, HEAD TABLE

10. CUPS AND SAUCERS, WATER GLASSES
11. HEAD TABLE
12. COFFEE, WATER GLASSES, ASH TRAYS
13. AFTER DINNER

CHAPTER 33
1. OMNIBUS
2. APPEARANCE
3. CLEARED, SOILED
4. ALERT
5. STOCKED
6. CRUMBS
7. STACK
8. SUPPLIES, TRAY
9. IN, OUT, EMPTY-HANDED
10. TURNOVER
11. REACH
12. BOTH
13. HAND, THE OTHER
14. TRAY, DIRECTION
15. GLASSES, 4
16. CUPS, SAUCERS?
17. SHOULDER, SUPPORT, BULK
18. BALANCE, TIP
19. TIME, STEP

CHAPTER 34
1. HOST-HOSTESS/SUPERVI-SOR
2. KINDNESS
3. EQUAL BASIS
4. AHEAD
5. GRANTED
6. SERVER
7. EQUAL
8. SINGLE DINNER
9. ENTRANCE
10. BE ALERT
11. PRIVATE
12. ONE

13. APPORTION
14. FAIR
15. ASSIGN
16. CUSTOMER SATISFACTION
17. OVERLOADED
18. IMPORTANT
19. SMILE
20. PUBLIC
21. "SUGGESTION" SELLING
22. 30
23. SUPER VISION

CHAPTER 35
1. BILL OF FARE
2. CRÊPE
3. ENTRÉE
4. À LA KING
5. GRATUITY
6. HOST
7. À LA CARTE
8. BON APPÉTIT
9. MAÎTRE D
10. ROUX
11. BOUILLABAISSE
12. CARTE DU JOUR
13. TABLE D'HÔTE
14. WINE LIST

1. BRAISE
2. PANFRY
3. BOIL
4. BLANCHE
5. PARBOIL
6. SAUTÉ
7. SCALD
8. WHIP
9. BLEND
10. MINCE

Comprehensive Server Test Answers

True and False
1. True
2. True
3. False
4. False
5. True
6. False
7. False
8. False
9. False
10. False
11. True
12. True
13. True
14. False
15. True
16. False
17. False
18. True
19. True
20. False
21. True
22. True
23. False
24. False
25. True

Fill in The Blanks
1. Dessert
2. Beverage
3. Waiting
4. Quickly
5. You
6. Serve
7. Service
8. One
9. Twelve
10. Hostess
11. Party Book
12. Omnibus
13. Balance
14. Tip
15. Supervisor/hostess/host
16. Private
17. One
18. Public
19. True
20. Tip
21. Pan-fry
22. Blend
23. Proud
24. Don't
25. Hot

Multiple Choice
1. C
2. A
3. B
4. B
5. A
6. 20
7. B
8. D
9. D
10. C
11. D
12. A
13. B

14. C   20. B
15. D   21. D
16. D   22. C
17. A   23. D
18. D   24. B
19. D   25. D

Circle the Correct Answer

1. Do say
2. Don't Say
3. Relax
4. Both
5. Playing Tennis
6. Repeat
7. Willingness/caring (both acceptable)
8. How is everything?
9. There anything else you need?
10. The tip goes down
11. Unless requested to do so by the guest
12. Self esteem/tips
13. Sales person
14. Have a nice day
15. It's been a pleasure serving you
16. Keep your eye on them in case they need additional service.
17. Please the guests
18 all three
19. from the girls
20. pour to the table
21. to assist the servers and guests
22. maintains a neat and clean personal appearance
23. provide supervision and leadership to insure guest satisfaction
24. Don't retaliate
25. Both

Index

bread and butter
    removing, 111
    serving, 59, 70, 110
buddy system, 10, 137
bussing tables, 159–62. *See also* trays
    duties at closing, 162
    duties off the floor, 161–62
    duties on the floor, 161
    job description for, 211–12
    origin of word, 159
    performance assessment form for, 213–14
    procedure for, 160
    tipping and, 160

C

champagne, opening, 104
charge accounts, handling, 130–31
checks. *See* guest checks
children, paying attention to, 9, 135–36, 168
cigarettes, 142
    lighting, 29, 142
cliques, 8
cocktails
    abbreviations for, 64, 65–66
    common, 65–66
    designating different, 138
    ordering, 62
    salesmanship and, 61–64
    script for, 192–93
    serving, 59, 62–63
    when serving multiple tables, 58–59
    writing order for, 86, 90
coffee. *See also* beverages
    refilling, 40, 118–19, 123, 148, 161, 195, 196, 200

knowledge of, 74
server as guest's guide through, 74
using abbreviations for items on, 74, 75, 84

N

napkin service, 36–37, 37

P

parties. *See* banquets and parties
performance assessment form
    for busser, 213–14
    for host-hostess/supervisor, 209–10
    for server, 205–206
personal problems, 7, 18
pointing to identify table, 18, 19
position system (for orders), 83, 91
    version I, 84, 85–89
    version II. *See* grid system (for orders)
promotions (for the restaurant), 143
psychology, 183–85
    in negative situations, 183–84
    for success, 184–85

R

removing items. *See* table, clearing
review of chapters
    busser, 162–63
    extra service, 139–40, 149–50
    host-hostess/supervisor, 171–72
    jargon, 180–81, 182
    preparation and technique, 44–46, 48–49, 54
    service as a profession, 12–13, 24–25

W

Knowledge is Power

To Earn More, You
Have to Learn More

**Service is an
Honorable Profession**